M000307536

INSEAD Business Press

Available titles:

Manfred F. R. Kets de Vries
TELLING FAIRY TALES IN THE BOARDROOM
How to Make Sure Your Organization Lives Happily Ever After

Manfred F. R. Kets de Vries
YOU WILL MEET A TALL, DARK STRANGER
Executive Coaching Challenges

Manfred F. R. Kets de Vries, Caroline Rook, Konstantin Korotov and Elizabeth Florent-Treacy
COACH AND COUCH 2nd EDITION
The Psychology of Making Better Leaders

Manfred F. R. Kets de Vries
SEX, MONEY, HAPPINESS AND DEATH (now available in paperback)
The Quest for Authenticity

Morten Bennedsen and Joseph Fan
THE FAMILY BUSINESS MAP
Assets and Roadblocks in Long Term Planning

Linda Brimm
GLOBAL COSMOPOLITANS
The Creative Edge of Difference

Lourdes Casanova
GLOBAL LATINAS
Latin America's Emerging Multinationals

Rolando Tomasini and Luk Van Wassenhove
HUMANITARIAN LOGISTICS

David Fubini, Colin Price and Maurizio Zollo
MERGERS
Leadership, Performance and Corporate Health

Manfred F. R. Kets de Vries
MINDFUL LEADERSHIP COACHING
Journeys into the Interior

James Teboul
SERVICE IS FRONT STAGE
Positioning Services for Value Management

Renato J. Orsato
SUSTAINABILITY STRATEGIES
When Does It Pay to Be Green?

J. Stewart Black and Allen J. Morrison
SUNSET IN THE LAND OF THE RISING SUN
Why Japanese Multinational Corporations Will Struggle in the Global Future

Michael McGannon and Juliette McGannon
THE BUSINESS LEADER'S HEALTH MANUAL
Tips and Strategies for Getting to the Top and Staying There

Manfred F. R. Kets de Vries, Konstantin Korotov and Elizabeth Florent-Treacy
THE COACHING KALEIDOSCOPE
Insights from the Inside

J. Frank Brown
THE GLOBAL BUSINESS LEADER
Practical Advice for Success in a Transcultural Marketplace

Jean-Claude Thoenig and Charles Waldman
THE MARKING ENTERPRISE
Business Success and Societal Embedding

Konstantin Korotov, Elizabeth Florent-Treacy, Manfred F. R. Kets de Vries and Andreas Bernhardt
TRICKY COACHING
Difficult Cases in Leadership Coaching

Frederic Godart
UNVEILING FASHION
Business, Culture, and Identity in the Most Glamorous Industry

INSEAD Business Press
Series Standing Order ISBN 978–0–230–01875–4 (hardback)
978–0–230–01876–1 (paperback)
(*outside North America only*)

You can receive future titles in this series as they are published by placing a standing order. Please contact your bookseller or, in case of difficulty, write to us at the address below with your name and address, the title of the series and the ISBN quoted above.

Customer Services Department, Macmillan Distribution Ltd, Houndmills, Basingstoke, Hampshire RG21 6XS, England

The Palgrave Kets de Vries Library

Manfred F. R. Kets de Vries, Distinguished Professor of Leadership Development and Organizational Change at INSEAD, is one of the world's leading thinkers on leadership, coaching, and the application of clinical psychology to individual and organizational change. Palgrave's professional business list operates at the interface between academic rigor and real-world implementation. Professor Kets de Vries's work exemplifies that perfect combination of intellectual depth and practical application and Palgrave is proud to bring almost a decade's worth of work together into the Palgrave Kets de Vries Library.

Sex, Money, Happiness, and Death
*The Coaching Kaleidoscope**
Mindful Leadership Coaching
Coach and Couch (2nd edition)[†]
You Will Meet a Tall, Dark Stranger
Telling Fairy Tales in the Boardroom

---

* Edited by Manfred F. R. Kets de Vries, Laura Guillén, Konstantin Korotov, Elizabeth Florent-Treacy
† Edited by Manfred F. R. Kets de Vries, Konstantin Korotov, Elizabeth Florent-Treacy, Caroline Rook

Telling Fairy Tales in the Boardroom

How to Make Sure Your Organization Lives Happily Ever After

Manfred F. R. Kets de Vries

Distinguished Clinical Professor of Leadership Development and Organizational Change, INSEAD, France, Singapore & Abu Dhabi

First published 2016 by
PALGRAVE MACMILLAN

Palgrave Macmillan in the UK is an imprint of Macmillan Publishers Limited, registered in England, company number 785998, of Houndmills, Basingstoke, Hampshire RG21 6XS.

Palgrave Macmillan in the US is a division of St Martin's Press LLC, 175 Fifth Avenue, New York, NY 10010.

Palgrave Macmillan is the global academic imprint of the above companies and has companies and representatives throughout the world.

Palgrave® and Macmillan® are registered trademarks in the United States, the United Kingdom, Europe and other countries.

ISBN 978–1–137–56272–2

This book is printed on paper suitable for recycling and made from fully managed and sustained forest sources. Logging, pulping and manufacturing processes are expected to conform to the environmental regulations of the country of origin.

A catalogue record for this book is available from the British Library.

A catalog record for this book is available from the Library of Congress.

Typeset by MPS Limited, Chennai, India.

*To Elisabet, who knows how to help children and adults
understand the true meaning of "living happily ever after."*

Contents

List of Figures / x

About the Author / xi

1   **Introduction** / 1

2   **White Raven, or The Leader Who No Longer
    Knew Himself** / 17

3   **The Bear-King, or The Price of Hubris** / 38

4   **The Kindly Crone, or How to Get the Best
    Out of People** / 62

5   **The Four Brothers, or How to Build an Effective Team** / 80

6   **King Lion, or How to Build an Effective Organization** / 102

7   **Happy Ever After** / 116

Bibliography / 121

Index / 123

List of Figures

2.1   The Johari Window matrix of self-knowledge ╱ 30

About the Author

Manfred F. R. Kets de Vries brings a different view to the much-studied subjects of leadership and the dynamics of individual and organizational change. Bringing to bear his knowledge and experience of economics (Econ. Drs., University of Amsterdam), management (ITP, MBA, and DBA, Harvard Business School), and psychoanalysis (Canadian Psychoanalytic Society, Paris Psychoanalytic Society, and the International Psychoanalytic Association), Kets de Vries scrutinizes the interface between international management, psychoanalysis, psychotherapy, dynamic psychiatry, and leadership coaching. His specific areas of interest are leadership, career dynamics, executive stress, entrepreneurship, family business, succession planning, cross-cultural management, high-performance team building, and the dynamics of corporate transformation and change.

Kets de Vries is the Distinguished Clinical Professor of Leadership Development and Organizational Change at INSEAD, France, Singapore, and Abu Dhabi. He was the Founder of INSEAD's Global Leadership Center, one of the largest leadership development centers in the world. In addition, he is program director of INSEAD's top management program, "The Challenge of Leadership: Developing Your Emotional Intelligence," and Scientific Director of the Executive Master's Program "Consulting and Coaching for Change" (and has five times received INSEAD's distinguished teacher award). He is also the Distinguished Visiting Professor of Leadership Development Research at the European School of Management and Technology (ESMT) in Berlin. He has held professorships at McGill University, the Ecole des Hautes Etudes Commerciales, Montreal, and the Harvard Business School, and he has lectured at management institutions around the world.

The Financial Times, Le Capital, Wirtschaftswoche, and *The Economist* have rated Manfred Kets de Vries among the world's leading leadership scholars. Kets de Vries is listed among the world's top 50 leading management thinkers and is among the most influential contributors to human resource management.

Kets de Vries is the author, co-author, or editor of more than 40 books, including *The Neurotic Organization; Leaders, Fools and Impostors; Life and Death in the Executive Fast Lane; The Leadership Mystique; The Happiness Equation; Are Leaders Born or Are They Made? The Case of Alexander the Great; The New Russian Business Leaders; Leadership by Terror: Finding Shaka Zulu in the Attic; The Global Executive Leadership Inventory; The Leader on the Couch; Coach and Couch; The Family Business on the Couch; Sex, Money, Happiness, and Death: The Quest for Authenticity; Reflections on Leadership and Character; Reflections on Leadership and Career; Reflections on Organizations; The Coaching Kaleidoscope; The Hedgehog Effect: The Secrets of High Performance Teams;* and *Mindful Leadership Coaching: Journeys into the Interior.* Two further books are in preparation.

In addition, Kets de Vries has published over 400 scientific papers as chapters in books and as articles. He has also written approximately 100 case studies, including seven that received the Best Case of the Year award. He is a regular contributor to a number of magazines. He writes blogs for the *Harvard Business Review* and *INSEAD Knowledge.* His work has been featured in such publications as *The New York Times, The Wall Street Journal, The Los Angeles Times, Fortune, BusinessWeek, The Economist, The Financial Times,* and *The International Herald Tribune.* His books and articles have been translated into 31 languages.

Kets de Vries is a member of 17 editorial boards and has been elected a Fellow of the Academy of Management. He is a founding member of the International Society for the Psychoanalytic Study of Organizations (ISPSO), which has honored him with a lifetime membership. Kets de Vries is also the first non-American recipient of the International Leadership Association Lifetime Achievement Award for his contributions to leadership research and development; he is considered one of the world's founding professionals in the development of leadership as a field and discipline. The American Psychological Association has honored him with the Harry and Miriam Levinson Award (Organizational Consultation division) for his contributions to the field of consultation. In the Netherlands, he has been awarded the Freud Award for his contributions at the interface of management and psychoanalysis. He has also received the Vision of Excellence Award from the Harvard Institute of Coaching. In addition, he is the recipient of two honorary doctorates.

Kets de Vries is a consultant on organizational design/transformation and strategic human resource management to leading US, Canadian, European, African, and Asian companies. As a global consultant in executive leadership development his clients have included ABB, ABN-AMRO, Accenture, Aegon, Air Liquide, Alcan, Alcatel, ATIC, Bain Consulting, Bang & Olufsen, Bonnier, BP, Cairn, Deutsche Bank, Ericsson, GE Capital, Goldman Sachs, Heineken, Hudson, HypoVereinsbank, Investec, KPMG, Lego, Liberty Life, Lufthansa, Lundbeck, McKinsey, National Australian Bank, Nokia, Novartis, Novo Nordisk, Origin, SABMiller, Shell, SHV, Spencer Stuart, Standard Bank of South Africa, Troika Dialog, Unilever, and Volvo Car Corporation. As an educator and consultant he has worked in more than 40 countries. In his role as a consultant, he is also the founder of the Kets de Vries Institute (KDVI), a boutique leadership development consulting firm.

The Dutch government has made him an Officer in the Order of Oranje Nassau. He was the first fly fisherman in Outer Mongolia and is a member of New York's Explorers Club. In his spare time he can be found in the rainforests or savannahs of Central Africa, the Siberian taiga, the Pamir and Altai Mountains, Arnhemland, or within the Arctic Circle.

Email: manfred.ketsdevries@insead.edu
www.ketsdevries.com
www.kdvi.com

Chapter 1

Introduction

Some day you will be old enough to start reading fairy tales again.

—C. S. Lewis

If you want your children to be intelligent, read them fairy tales. If you want them to be more intelligent, read them more fairy tales.

—Albert Einstein

Fairy tales since the beginning of recorded time, and perhaps earlier, have been a means to conquer the terrors of mankind through metaphor.

—Jack Zipes

Once we are destined to live out our lives in the prisons of our mind, our one duty is to furnish it well.

—Peter Ustinov

Introduction

We all know where we are with a fairy story. There is a cast of predictable characters (handsome prince, wicked stepmother, beautiful princess, the odd dragon, frog, or otherwise cursed beast, and so on). Our hero or heroine is submitted to terrible trials, cruelty, and injustice, but in the end the baddies get their comeuppance, good triumphs, and everyone lives happily ever after.

Knowing or anticipating the familiar framework of a story means that we absorb the learning it contains quickly; our mind is open to the message and not distracted or preoccupied by the structure of the tale. In this way, numerous traditional stories and fairy tales provide a shortcut to a moral lesson and reflections on human behavior. Their usefulness as a literary and psychological device has been recognized since the earliest times and has been perpetuated throughout our oral and written literary history, from Aesop's Fables in 600 BCE, to the moral tales of La Fontaine in the 17th century and the Brothers Grimm in the 19th, and to the pantomime tradition in British theater, which continues to be universally popular. These archetypal tales, with their immediately recognizable dramatics, characters and fundamental moral truths, are the rootstock of most world fiction and drama, embedded in our ancestral human history. They transcend pure entertainment and, because they involve the reader or listener imaginatively, they appeal to our secret selves. This resonance enables storytellers to fulfill their basic therapeutic function—to reflect our deepest fears and desires and help us integrate them into a healthy personality.

In this book I have written new fairy tales for what may seem on first consideration an unlikely audience—senior executives and leaders of organizations, and the people who work with them as coaches. Some might consider this an eccentric enterprise. All I can say in response is that everyone likes a story—and fairy tales more than most—not least because we are all in the process of constructing our own story, the narrative of our own life. All coaching, psychotherapeutic, and psychoanalytical inter-ventions begin with the request for the client to tell their story. For the five stories in this book I have borrowed the format of traditional fairy tales and used it to dramatize five key themes of dysfunctional or doomed leadership. This guise is an excellent means of transmitting messages that might otherwise fall on resolutely deaf ears.

The accompanying commentaries analyze the situational basis of each tale and the ways in which it is analogous to leadership behavior and organizational culture (effective or otherwise). This diagnostic element is supported by a real-life vignette that illustrates an occasion when I encountered dysfunctional executive behavior and how the situation was handled. A self-assessment test after each tale reinforces the main lessons and guides the reader's interpretation of the results.

The stimulus for this little book of fairy tales for executives was an invitation to do a TED talk. These have a very different format from the speeches I am used to giving at conferences and so on. There's no time to ramble. You have to stick to the point, as you have a maximum of 19 minutes for your talk. My presentations are usually much longer because I like to tell stories—and I also like to engage in dialogue with my audience when I give presentations.

I was bothered about how to present the essence of what I wanted to say within such a limited amount of time. But the major headache the time limitation gave me was also a blessing, as the challenge forced me to review the way I give presentations. The TED talk taught me something about the essence of storytelling.

What would be the best way to get what I wanted to say across? What did I want the audience to retain? What messages did I want them to take away from my stories? That last question made me think of fairy tales. Nearly all fairy tales contain a specific, hidden message. Fairy tales teach life lessons, reveal human foibles, and are very often highly moralistic. Like Molière's Monsieur Jourdain in his play *Le Bourgeois Gentilhomme*, who says that "for years now I've been speaking in prose without knowing it," the TED talk challenge made me realize that all my life—in my work as a management professor, psychoanalyst, consultant, and executive coach—I had been telling fairy tales. Perhaps I should take the opportunity to do it more deliberately.

Fairy tales have always had a great attraction for me. As a child, I devoured one volume of fairy tales after another. I could never get enough of the stories. Now, I had a chance to configure a number of fairy tales for adults, for a specific purpose. But what sort of fairy tales would appeal to executives and hold meaning for them?

Storytelling is a universal phenomenon. The cultures in which we live largely consist of the stories people have told about their experiences. Storytelling has always given us a window into our evolutionary history. Since the beginning of time, storytelling has been a community act that involves sharing knowledge and values—a form of communication that evolved along with the human species. Before most people could read or write, the stories told at firesides and in village market places were the way our predecessors handed down laws and values, religious beliefs, taboos, knowledge, and wisdom. Communicating through stories has been one of the most unifying themes in the history of humankind. Before the eighteenth century, in particular, fairy tales were a common source of entertainment for both adults and children—an essential part of daily life.

The stories told dealt with basic life events, especially coming-of-age processes and the emotional ups and downs associated with them. Stories were highly effective ways of mastering the psychological conflicts that humans face. Birth, death, marriage, love, hate, fear, joy, wickedness, forgiveness, rejection, and acceptance were regular themes.

Because these stories dealt with the most basic elements of human existence, the same types of story were passed down by word of mouth from generation to generation over widely divergent cultures and periods in time. The similarity of these stories reflects the underlying group dynamics that are shared by all cultures. Just as stories about strange real-life experiences are told and re-told, the classic fairy tales familiar to most societies came into being through the same tradition of repetition. In spite of many variations, the main themes of these stories remained very much the same.

Fairy tales and fables form part of our collective cultural heritage, capturing the most extreme forms of human drama and emotions. They are also the metaphoric reflections of significant events. Storytelling enabled our ancestors to survive and thrive, as the stories reflected psychic realities and lived experiences. Their stories helped them navigate the dangers surrounding them, often demonstrating the triumph of the small and weak over the large and powerful. In that respect, these stories can also be seen as tales full of hope. They are also moral tales, presenting basic human values. More often than not, generosity and kindness are rewarded in these stories, while greed and cruelty are punished.

Storytelling has not lost its value as a fundamental human activity, even in our digital age. The stories that reflect our cultural heritage are as relevant today as they were generations ago. Through them we tap into the wisdom of the collective unconscious that derives from our ancestors' cultural heritage. Influenced by these stories, and guided by the archetypal characters represented in them, we can figure out what kind of people we are, and what kind we would like to be.

Stories of this kind touch us in more ways than we can fathom, so that even in contemporary society, we are constantly drawn back to ancient parables, fables, and fairy tales, reworking them in modern contexts. There is a sense of cultural communality, in that the modern teller of a tale, by telling it, is linked to everyone who has told such stories before.

Many of us fail to realize the extent to which stories influence our behavior and shape our culture. Yet even though we may not be aware of it, stories drive everything we do—how we think about our past, decide on our present, plan for our future, regulate our conduct, and even define our personalities. We gain a sense of who we are by listening to stories, telling others stories and building an interior narrative about the things that happen to us. From the point of view of human development, each of us is a storyteller at heart. We are the heroes and heroines of our own life narratives. Stories help us to find our way through the maze that is our life's journey. They are beacons of certainty in a sea of turmoil.

The themes of traditional fairy tales and the way they are constructed dramatize the issues that preoccupy us. Each character in these stories portrays a state or condition of our own nature, consciousness, and emotional and spiritual development. We engage our imagination when telling or listening to a story, and begin to develop thoughts, opinions, and ideas that align with those of the storyteller. In this way we step out of our own shoes, see things differently, and experience empathy with the hero or heroine of the story. Because of this, the stories we hear can have a powerful influence on our beliefs and moral values.

Our identification with the protagonists in traditional tales is simplified by their one-dimensional characterization. They are simple, clever, ugly, beautiful, poor, rich, wicked, or kind-hearted. Precisely because these tales do not explore deeper dimensions of human experience and relationships, they gain in clarity. Not only are their descriptions rather superficial, the heroes, heroines, and villains of these tales are usually also nameless (maiden, woodsman, goblin, king, queen, big bad wolf), or given token names (Jack, Snow White, Prince Charming, Wicked Stepmother). The illusion created is that the hero or heroine could be any one of us, and that strange and wondrous things can happen to all of us.

The magic of these tales is built on abstraction. They have non-specific settings (the forest, a castle, a land far, far away), polarized characters (entirely good or entirely evil) and most importantly take place "once upon a time," which needs no further precision. All these things are instantly understood by us. Their lasting appeal attests to their richness and effectiveness as methods of symbolic and artistic communication.

Most of us first encounter traditional tales in childhood, but in fact they are far from being stories just for children. They are encoded with spiritual and moral lessons for all of us. They help us understand that conflict is followed by some kind of resolution; they teach us that there is always a way out. In this way, they provide us with a safety net. Through fairy tales, we form a concept of how the world works and what our place in this world should be.

The fairy tale

Fairy tales have always played a prominent role within the storytelling tradition. They are one of humankind's most important sense-making mechanisms. They explore the boundaries between reality and fantasy and between the animate and inanimate world. In fairy tales, the most amazing things happen: animals talk; people turn into animals; fairies are helpers; goblins create mischief; dragons and other monsters lie in wait for us; and there are miracles just around the corner. When we enter these "other worlds," there is the expectation that we will return to our own world with a new awareness, and with a new sense of energy and hope.

The perception that fairy tales are intended for the young is relatively new and has been reinforced by the Disney effect. These sanitized cartoon versions of classic fairy tales have stripped the originals of much of their complexity and sensuality and in the process lost a considerable amount of their symbolism. Most of us are unaware of the darkness of many versions of these tales, having been dazzled by the Technicolor versions with which we are familiar.

Fairy tales are one result of our struggle to control the bestial and barbaric forces that are part of the human condition through metaphors and symbolic narrative. They are the closets in which we keep our deepest secrets and fears. Think how many fairy tales dramatize some of our worst fears: abandonment, sibling rivalry, starvation, cannibalism, murder, rape, and incest. It's no wonder that the fairy tales we are told as children mark us for life. But reading or listening to these tales allows us to work through these fears and learn about what's right and what's wrong. From an evolutionary psychological point of view, fairy tales may have been a developmental necessity, enabling us to master the challenges that life had in store for us.

Structural patterns

Most fairy tales start with the protagonist leading an ordinary, unremarkable life. To add to the sense of drama, our hero or heroine may have had an inauspicious start in life, being poor, bereaved, abandoned, imprisoned, mocked, or pitied. Yet he or she may be yearning for something more—an idea that we can all identify with. Early in the tale, the hero or heroine receives a "call" to bid goodbye to this dull life and embark on something exciting but unknown. Frequently the protagonist resists, but the pressure is on: the "call" cannot be ignored. Once the protagonist answers the call, there is often a period of preparation.

The time has come for the protagonist's heroic journey, away from humdrum daily life to a land of adventure, trials, and magical rewards. Crossing the threshold into this other world is about taking risks and pursuing a quest. The hero or heroine is tasked with performing an extraordinary feat—like slaying a dragon or spinning a room full of straw into gold.

At this point in the tale, our protagonists face life-threatening dangers— journeys through pitch-black forests surrounded by wolves and bears, across treacherous mountains, or over endless deserts—or have to make superhuman efforts to fulfill their destiny. They encounter dragons, giants, goblins, wizards, witches, and trolls. Fortunately, however, the very act of crossing a dangerous threshold attracts helpers in the form of fairy godmothers, kind strangers, and animal guides, who may appear in disguise. These guides or mentors help our protagonists overcome the dangers they encounter and succeed in their quest. (In the fairy tales I recount in this book, our heroes and heroines will meet mentors and helpers in the form of a white raven, a stranger, an old crone, and the master teachers of four brothers.)

The most intense and dramatic part of the journey—the trial—has now arrived. The ability of our protagonists to complete the quest is challenged. To pass these tests, they must draw on the skills and insights they have gained on their journey. They will emerge triumphant, as transformed individuals.

In all these fairy tales, the protagonists survive not just the perils of the magic world but those encountered on their journey into their inner world. The figures and imagery in the tales—the wicked stepmother, fairy godmother, darkness, forest dangers, magic mirrors—may symbolize disturbing inner emotional states. Having overcome various challenges, very similar to rites of passage, the protagonists metaphorically "return" to the place where they started. They re-enter the "old" world, but they have changed profoundly. Things will never be the same again.

Many fairy tales can be interpreted as dramatizations of our inner darkness, allowing us to acknowledge and confront it. The deep, dark, dangerous forests where we get lost stand for the near-impenetrable world of our unconscious. Although the dark forest is an unknown place, inhabited by wild things, it is also a place of opportunity and transformation where we will find our true selves.

Then there is the happy ever after. Often the first glimmering of hope comes at the very apex of catastrophe in these tales. When all hope seems lost, the prince arrives, the villain makes a mistake, or the heroine returns from the dead. In fairy tales, there is a reward in the end, the humiliation or death of the villain, marriage to a prince or princess, and kingdoms or treasure to be granted.

The hope for transformation

If there is one clear constant in the fairy tale, it is transformation. These tales demonstrate that change is possible if we prepare ourselves for it properly. Personal transformation is one of the key themes in fairy tales. All the main characters in the most famous tales are transformed in one way or another. If we feel ugly, we can become beautiful. If we feel powerless, we can become powerful. We may be poor, but we can become rich. This kind of polarity is a characteristic of fairy tales.

The real power in these tales lies in the narrative device that goodness conquers evil, and that even the darkest experiences and greatest setbacks will lead to a "happy ever after." The protagonists in these stories overcome all challenges and trials and become wiser, stronger, and able to deal with every kind of danger. Fairy tales teach us that if we are smart, honest, generous, modest, and kind, we will succeed even when it seems all hope is gone; that transformation is possible for all of us.

To illustrate this point, let's look at one of the most famous fairy tales, Cinderella. This poor girl endures the direst circumstances—neglected by her father, starved, abused and bullied by her stepmother and stepsisters, forced to drudge for everyone—yet a miracle occurs and the drudge is transformed from a downtrodden domestic into a captivating princess and the cherished bride of the prince. The incidental *schadenfreude* of her sisters' humiliation sharpens the delight of the tale. This dynamic occurs frequently—beasts and frogs are transformed into handsome princes; snow babies become real, live children. These tales suggest that everyone, no matter how humble, can be elevated. No wonder that such a message has universal appeal. No wonder that we all love fairy tales, with their suggestion that similar magic is just around the corner for us. If fairy tales do their job properly, they help us to lose ourselves in another world where we experience a sense of wonder, mystery, and excitement in such a way that we return to our day-to-day world transformed for the better.

Symbolism and dream imagery

Fairy tales help us understand that there's more to reality than meets the eye and a world of illusion and fantasy beneath the world as we see it. These tales convey subliminal messages about the universal truths—good and evil, light and darkness, happiness and sorrow—that lie at the core of the human experience.

While these tales have never been intended solely for children, their content has immediate appeal for them. Children—as our prehistoric ancestors did—engage in magical thinking. They clearly relate to ideas like wish fulfilment, talking animals, and supernatural beings, which are integral elements of many fairy tales. To a child, anything is possible and the boundary between fantasy and reality is highly permeable. The child who identifies with a hero who performs magical deeds is compensating in fantasy for the limitations of his own young body. Repeated exposure to such fantasies supports the belief that as the child grows up, his or her persistence in overcoming obstacles will be rewarded.

The symbolism in fairy tales is sometimes quite subtle or extremely sub-liminal; on other occasions its rawness is very obvious. The psychoanalyst Carl Jung viewed fairy tales as the purest and simplest expression of psy-chic processes of the collective unconscious, as they represent archetypes in their simplest, barest, and most concise form. Deep dark woods full of wild animals are common representations of feared or negative elements within us, the unexplored side of our nature that can be dangerous and chaotic—elements that sometimes surface in nightmares. Jung insisted that something valuable might emerge from these dark places. This wild side of our nature is an important and in some ways the most creative part of us. Our challenge, however, is to integrate this side into our identity in a constructive way.

Some experiences in life seem like setbacks or hang over us like dark clouds, and our first reaction is to wish to avoid them. However, with hindsight, we may come to realize that these experiences have been extremely valuable. They might have forced us to develop aspects of ourselves that we had neglected or to enter the wild places in our inner world that we had consciously or unconsciously avoided. In these wild places we also meet the frog prince, the wise old man, the goose that lays golden eggs, the wolf disguised as a sweet old grandmother, the murderous giant, the evil goblin, and the cannibalistic witch. But for their early audiences, this symbolism was reinforced by the very real nature of the dark forests that are the setting for so many of these tales. Beyond the safety of the fires around which the storyteller and listeners sat, the dangers of the forest were palpable, from thieves and bandits lying in wait for unsuspecting travelers, to bears and wolves hungry for a kill.

There has always been a great deal of communality between dreams and fairy tales. From an evolutionary psychological perspective, fairy tales, like dreams, might help us rehearse for the dangers we encounter in real life. If something weighs heavily on our mind during the day, the chances are that we will dream about it, either specifically or through symbolic imagery. Dreams are a form of private theater that enables us to solve problems more effectively while we are asleep than when awake—in a dream state we make connections more quickly than when we are awake, and there is less conscious censorship. Fairy tales perform a similar function: they are a kind of collective theater, enacting dramas that we all recognize and share and that help us remain sane.

Like dreams that scare us but also prepare us for the realities of life, fairy tales warn us about the dangers we may encounter during our journey.

They tell us not to give in to temptation, not to trust liars, and not to underestimate others. In this way, fairy tales and dreams fulfill an important societal function. They give us experiences we can't have in real life, in particular situations that could be dangerous or problematic, and teach us how to avoid them.

Repetition can be a great healer. Just as our subconscious might trigger recurring dreams in the process of arriving at some form of problem resolution, our human impulse toward repetition may also explain why we are attracted to certain fairy tales. The particular conflicts we are trying to master may be the reason why we feel compelled to listen to specific tales over and over again. We may be trying to find ways to deal with the dark and terrible forces that are part of us. Even today, there are still symbolic dragons to be slain, wizards and witches creating magic, and quests to be undertaken.

Whatever our culture, fairy tales teach us valuable life lessons. They put ordinary people in extraordinary situations. Their depictions of miraculous events, encounters, and experiences remain a valid part of the human experience. They are an invaluable part of our shared and personal history. With their symbolic language, the fairy tales that we first encounter in childhood retain their power over us, even as adults.

The fairy tale in the leader's journey

Spiritual growth is at the heart of every fairy tale: as the protagonists leave their (happy or troubled) home to face and eventually triumph over difficult challenges, they are expected to develop their highest potential. Leaders face similar dilemmas. In many ways, leaders can be viewed as the heroes and heroines of contemporary fairy tales, given the fantasies we tend to project onto people in positions of power and authority.

Many of the life lessons provided in fairy tales illustrate the major "dangers" of leadership. One of the most famous is Hans Christian Andersen's tale *The Emperor's New Clothes*. The Emperor in this tale is like many of the leaders we encounter. They can be intimidating, even frightening, but when we study them more carefully, we realize that their power and authority have no substance—they are like the emperor who has no clothes. In another example, the Wicked Queen in the tale of Snow White is like an aging leader struggling with generational envy, unable to let go. Fairy tales can be read as maps of success and failure—how to live as safely and happily as possible, and how to avoid making fatal mistakes when taking decisions.

Effective organizational and political leaders should be able to take care of the basics: they need to help their people make a living, direct them to overcome the competition or enemy, and maintain harmony within the organization or society. They are merchants of hope. They speak to the collective imagination of their people to create a group identity. Conversely, dysfunctional leaders will lead their organization or society into chaos, their people into misery and hardship, and bring discord and indiscipline.

Fairy tales can be used as a medium to decipher the conundrums faced by leaders and give us a rich opportunity to explore potentially conflict-ridden issues. They can be highly illustrative ways of learning how to deal with the challenges of an executive's world. These stories can have a much greater impact than the content of many conventional books on leadership, most of which send us to sleep rather than having the power to delight or touch us and teach us universal truths. Fairy tales help us imprint pictures of effective and dysfunctional leadership on our minds.

Fairy tales are also more likely to stimulate our imagination, clarify emotions, and suggest solutions to problems and anxieties. The roles of king, queen, prince, princess, and others can become avatars for the challenges faced by people in leadership positions. There are also similarities between events in the world of fairy tales and what happens in organizational life (quests, challenges, glittering prizes, succession issues, battles to be fought). Presenting the dilemmas of leadership in the form of fairy tales can be a very powerful catalyst to help leaders change—because, as we have seen, fairy tales always have human transformation at their core.

Storytelling is also an extremely powerful weapon in a leader's arsenal. Using their people as an audience for their stories, leaders can illustrate the kind of challenges they are up against, convince them to take a certain path, and illustrate the consequences of good and bad behavior. Like the heroes and heroines in fairy tales, stories inform people in leadership positions that they must first focus on managing themselves before managing others, and learn to think differently about the ways people in organizations affect each other. As leaders learn to manage their own anxiety, they can handle themselves more calmly and lead even in difficult times.

The five deadly dangers of leadership

In my TED talk, when I wanted to present the essence of leadership I decided to recount five fairy tales to highlight the most deadly dangers that I believe executives face. What are the things they really need to attend to? What are the biggest pitfalls they face? This book extends that device. The five tales here address a number of fundamental issues associated with the leadership mystique and are written to make executives aware of the dangers they will encounter on their various quests.

Why do some leaders succeed and others derail? What differentiates effective and ineffective leaders? The first danger many leaders are prone to is lack of self-knowledge.

The second danger is hubris. Many leaders become too arrogant and lose touch with reality. Why do so many leaders self-destruct in this way?

The third danger is a leader's inability to get the best out of people. Ineffective leaders fail to stretch the people who work for them. They don't know how to make people better than they think that they can be.

Linked to this danger is the fourth and greater danger, which is a leader's inability to create well-functioning teams. Effective leaders are aware of and accept their personal limitations and surround themselves with people who have the strengths they lack, creating executive role constellations of people with complementary characteristics.

The fifth danger is creating a gulag—what is it that prevents leaders building great places to work?

In this book I attempt to dramatize these five deadly dangers through the traditional medium of fairy tales. None of us is ever too old to believe in the magic of these stories, which continue to resonate in the human psyche. I believe even the most hardened executives will find it difficult to resist the pull of the alternative worlds described in these tales. Fairy tales provide an encouraging model for living, reminding us unconsciously of life's positive possibilities. The "happy ever after" is not a conclusion, but a doorway to a more hopeful reality. These tales not only teach us lessons about the external world, but also give us the opportunity to embark on an inner journey.

The messages in these fairy tales can be seen as warnings of what can go wrong for people in a leadership position. However, they are also intended to inspire hope and the belief that something better can be achieved. All these tales deal with the dos and don'ts of leadership. I hope leaders will read these tales with fresh eyes and open ears. I hope that the fact of having picked up this book means that they are prepared to learn what they can do better.

Fairy tales have always been about getting through the worst of what life throws at us. As human beings, we have to face pain, boredom, sadness, and fear. Our need to compensate for this is translated into instinctive activities like fantasy and storytelling. The stories we tell ourselves help us deal with the human condition. May we never grow too old to believe in the magic of those tales.

I assume, if you are reading a book of fairy tales for executives, that you are familiar with organizational life, its good and bad aspects, the pleasures when it works well, and the misery when it becomes dysfunctional. As you read, I would like you to reflect on your responses to each tale. How does the tale make you feel? Is there something in the story that strikes a chord? Do you recognize any of the characters? Do you recognize any of the challenges? Does your organization seem as if it is under a wicked spell? Or is your place of work on track to its happy ever after? Following each tale, I provide a real-life (anonymized) example of how I observed a similar crisis or situation in an organizational context, and what the outcome was. At the end of each chapter, you will find a self-assessment test, which will enable you to gauge how you rate on the spectrum of each of the deadly dangers dramatized in these tales.

chapter 2

White Raven, or The Leader Who No Longer Knew Himself

"He who knows others is wise; he who knows himself is enlightened."

—*Lao Tzu*

"The first thing you have to know is yourself. A man who knows himself can step outside himself and watch his own reactions like an observer."

—*Adam Smith*

"You need to know things the others don't know. It's what no one knows about you that allows you to know yourself."
—*Don DeLillo*

"You are here on earth to unearth who on earth you are."
—*Eric Michael Leventhal*

Once upon a time there was a wise king, so beloved by his people, and so respected by all the neighboring kingdoms, that he was generally regarded as the greatest monarch alive. Under his rule, industry and fine arts flourished. The workers prospered and everyone was happy.

Now, it was well known that the king had a magic mirror that helped him rule so well. Every morning when he arose, the king would stand before the mirror. As he gazed at his reflection he could see his strengths and weaknesses; he could see his feet set firmly on the ground; he saw the problems he had to face and how to solve them; he saw the things that mattered and the things that were unimportant; he saw the decisions he had to take and how to take them. When he turned away from the mirror, the king felt confident that he would rule his kingdom justly, kindly, and wisely.

But not everyone in the kingdom was happy. Deep in a cave in the darkest forest lived a wicked goblin that was eaten up with envy that the king was so adored by his subjects. As time went on, and the people grew happier, healthier, and wealthier, the goblin's hatred grew and grew.

One day, while the king was visiting his people in a distant part of the land, the wicked goblin crept into the palace, entered the king's bedroom, and put the magic mirror under a wicked spell. Laughing loudly, it said to itself, "Now let's see how the king rules his kingdom!"

The next morning, the king awoke and went to the mirror as usual. But when he looked at the glass, something dreadful happened. He no longer recognized his reflection. Everything was distorted and confused. "Is this what I am really like?" the king asked himself. "Is this my real self? Were all the other reflections false?" Day after day the mirror reflected someone who was a stranger to him. The king began to lose confidence in himself. He was very unhappy. He started to question the decisions he had made and changed his mind again and again, no longer sure that what he was doing was right. The king's confusion and doubt spread throughout the court. People began to wonder what had happened to their ruler. Now instead of being just, wise, and benevolent he seemed weak, insecure, and erratic. The discontent within the kingdom was music to the ears of the wicked goblin.

But after a while the king's subjects became used their ruler's changed behavior. They said, "Things may not be as good as they were but they could be worse. Just look at the way other kingdoms are governed! Compared with them, we are not too badly off." This made the goblin very angry.

One day, when the king was in the throne room with his counselors, the goblin crept once more into the royal bedchamber, stole the magic mirror, and took it to the highest mountain in the land. At the summit, it held the mirror above its head, uttered a second spell, and threw it down the steepest cliff. When the mirror hit the ground it broke into millions of tiny pieces, which the wind picked up, blowing fragments of the cursed mirror into the eyes of every man, woman, and child in the kingdom.

From that moment on, all the king's subjects saw a distorted view of the world, as even the smallest fragment retained the power of the cursed mirror. With these chips of glass in their eyes, the king's people lost their sense of who they were. Like the king, they became strangers to themselves.

Faster than seemed possible, the kingdom, which had been known for its wise, considerate, and just rule, became a chaotic, unhappy place in which everyone had lost their grip on reality. The people no longer knew right from wrong. Where there had been harmony there was now discord, where happiness, sorrow. Gloating over the misery it had caused, the wicked goblin laughed and laughed until its belly shook.

Now a stranger to himself, the king's mood grew dark and somber and he withdrew more and more from his people. His despondency was contagious. Nobody laughed and people grew suspicious of their neighbors. They lost all sense of purpose and forgot how to do their work properly.

One night, the king had a terrifying dream. In his dream, he looked into the magic mirror and the sight of his own face filled him with dread. As he gazed in horror at his reflection, the mirror started to shake. It cracked into a million pieces that were whipped by a strong wind into a dark cloud that was blown high in the sky and from somewhere came the sound of malicious laughter. The king woke up, bathed in sweat, and summoned all his courtiers, crying, "Tell me the meaning of this terrible dream!" But none of his attendants could give him a satisfactory answer.

His courtiers' inability to help made the king even more despondent. With the horror of the dream still deeply etched in his mind, the king invited the wisest people in his kingdom to help him solve the riddle. But none of them could find the answer.

Finally, one of the courtiers told the king about a wise woman who lived in a land far, far away, and was known for her great knowledge. "Who knows?" the courtier said hesitantly. "She might be the one who will solve the riddle of your dream. She might be able to help you." When the king heard these words, he sent his most capable knight to fetch the wise woman, saying, "Ride day and night, and do whatever it takes, but bring this woman to my court without delay."

When the wise woman arrived at the court, the king recounted his dream. The woman listened carefully, then said, "Sire, the dream shows that someone has put a terrible curse on your kingdom."

"What can I do to make the kingdom well again?" demanded the king. "What can I do to recapture what we once had?" The woman replied, "The only way to break this spell is to find the potion of truth. But this will be a very difficult quest. It is only found in a far-off land. Anyone who tries to obtain it will be faced with grave dangers. Many have tried, but all have failed."

While the wise woman was speaking, the king's two sons were listening carefully. Now they stepped forward and said, "Please, father, give us your blessing to search for this rare potion. We will be honored to serve you and save the kingdom."

The king was very touched by their words, but feared to lose his sons on such a dangerous expedition. Still they continued to beg him to let them go. Finally, the king consented, and said, "Go, and my blessings upon the two of you. Because your quest is so important to everyone in our kingdom, the one who brings back this magic potion will be anointed as my successor."

Without delay, the two princes saddled their horses and galloped away. They journeyed night and day, crossing lakes, valleys, mountains, and other wild places in search of the magic potion.

The further the brothers went from the kingdom, the more clear-sighted they became, as the spell of the evil goblin began to lose its power. One day, completely exhausted from a long day's riding, they arrived at a crossing where two roads met. One road was wide, straight, and clear, while the other was narrow and overgrown. At the crossing was a sign that read:

> Foolish traveler, beware!
> Continue only if you dare.
> Take the straight path: you might return.
> The other's dangers you will learn.

The older prince said hastily, "I'll take the straight path," and before his brother could say a word, he galloped away. The younger prince realized that his brother had taken advantage of him, but he had no choice and took the narrow, overgrown way.

As night fell, the older prince arrived at a superb castle. He was very thankful to have reached such a place, as he was truly exhausted. As he dismounted, he was greeted warmly by people who lit his way with torches. They took his horse, and guided him through the entrance, which was richly decorated with precious stones and beautiful paintings. The prince was enchanted by such a reception after the hardships of his journey. "Finally," he thought, "I will be able to rest." But alas for the prince—what he did not know was that the beautiful castle was an illusion. In reality, he was in the wicked goblin's lair.

The prince entered a sumptuous hall, full of the sound of music and delicious smells. The tables were laden with so much food and wine that they were on the verge of collapsing. The prince fell on the food and drink hungrily. All around, beautiful women cast seductive glances at him and continued to fill his plate and glass.

The wicked goblin, disguised as a noble lord, welcomed him and gave him all the honors the prince could have wished for. Before long the prince had forgotten all about his quest for the magic potion. He felt very sleepy. "I never want to leave this wonderful place," he thought.

Meanwhile, the younger prince had taken the narrow, overgrown path and was on a very different journey. He traveled through snow-covered mountain passes, arid deserts, dangerous swamps, and treacherous rivers, but, in spite of all the hardships, he pressed on. The promise he had made to his father weighed heavily on his mind. He was determined to complete the quest, whatever the cost.

Whenever the prince met people, he would ask them, "Tell me, please, where I can find the potion of truth." Every time, the answer was, "Far away, in a distant land, in a place where many dangers await you." But despite these discouraging replies, the prince did not give up.

One day, as the prince was riding through a deep, dark wood he heard a strange cry. After a long search, he came upon a beautiful white raven caught in a snare. To his great surprise, the bird spoke to him: "Please, my prince, set me free. An evil goblin has trapped me in this snare and if it finds me it will kill and eat me."

The prince, who was very kind at heart, freed the bird. The white raven spread its wings and prepared to fly but as it did so said, "Dear prince, I am for ever in your debt. You have saved my life. Is there anything that I can do for you? Let me know your heart's desire." The prince said, "Please help me to find the potion of truth. I have looked for it far and wide, but it is nowhere to be found."

The raven replied, "Dear prince, I will help you but you must listen very carefully. Not far from here, in the deepest part of this dark, dangerous wood, you will find a castle. You should enter this castle but beware. The castle is just an illusion. In truth, it's the lair of a wicked goblin. This goblin has caused me great suffering and is responsible for the misery that has visited your father's kingdom. Therefore, be cautious. Do not eat or drink anything you are offered or you will fall into a deep sleep and be unable to complete your quest. When everyone is asleep tonight, I will come and find you. I will lead you to a magic sword that is the only weapon that can kill the goblin. You must cut off its head, and then you will find the potion of truth among its treasure in the cave."

When the prince arrived at the castle, it was just as the white raven had told him. Delicious food and wine was put before him, but the prince only pretended to eat and drink. The same beautiful women smiled at him, but the prince just smiled back. After a while, the prince lay down and pretended to be fast asleep.

When the castle was completely silent the prince heard the sound of wings and the white raven appeared. As it had promised, the bird guided him to the magic sword, which the prince fastened to his belt. Then he followed the raven into the depths of the cave, from which strange sounds were coming. It was the evil goblin, fast asleep and snoring loudly. With one great thrust of the sword the prince cut off its ugly head. The raven then flew to a shelf in the farthest corner, where the prince found the phial containing the potion of truth. As he put it safely in his pack, he heard desperate cries and loud banging even deeper in the cave. There he found his unfortunate brother, imprisoned in a dungeon. Another great thrust of the magic sword sliced through the heavy lock and the brothers fell into one another's arms.

Saying farewell to the white raven, the two princes set off on the long journey home. But as they traveled, the older prince grew more and more quiet and withdrawn. He was deeply ashamed that he had fallen for the evil goblin's tricks and failed in the quest to find the potion of truth. Now, he remembered what their father had said as he gave them his blessing: his younger brother would inherit the kingdom.

His heart was torn with envy. As they got nearer to the kingdom, the older prince determined to kill his brother and steal the potion. He would tell his father that his brother had died bravely, but that he was the one who had successfully completed the quest. He would be named the future king. As they drew close to home, the older prince looked for an opportunity to murder his brother and take the magic phial.

One day, as they rested near a well, the older prince saw that his chance had come. He told his brother that he could hear a raven calling from deep in the well. His brother said he could hear nothing. "Come closer to the well," said the older prince. The younger prince approached but could still hear nothing. "I fear it is our friend the white raven," said the older prince. At this, the younger prince ran to the well and leaned over to try to see the bird. As he did so, his brother pushed him as hard as he could and the poor prince tumbled in. Without looking back, the older prince took the potion from his brother's pack, jumped on his horse, and rode towards the kingdom.

When he reached the castle, the first thing his father asked was, "Where is your brother? Why isn't he here? What happened to him?"

"Alas, father," said the prince, "we came to a crossing and my brother took the way of no return. After we parted, I saw him no more. But despite the many hardships that lay before me, I succeeded in obtaining the potion of truth."

On hearing this news, the king cried with joy that the spell that hung over the kingdom could now be broken. But he also shed many tears over the loss of his younger son, and cherished the secret hope that he might still be alive.

And indeed he was. The well into which he had been pushed was dry, and filled with soft leaves that broke his fall. For many hours the younger prince called for help, hoping that a passing traveler might hear him. After some time, a traveler did stop by, hoping to water his horse. When he heard the desperate cries coming from deep in the well, he lowered a rope, and helped the prince out. Thanking his rescuer from the bottom of his heart, the younger prince went on his way to the kingdom.

When he arrived at his father's castle, there was great joy throughout the land. But the king turned red with anger when the prince told his father how his older brother had robbed him of the potion and tried to kill him. "How could he do such a vile thing to his brother?" cried the king. "He will die for this."

But the young prince pleaded with his father to spare his brother's life and eventually softened the old man's heart. Instead, the older prince was banished from the kingdom. Where he went, nobody knew—and nobody ever cared.

The king told the prince what the wise woman had decreed should be done with the potion of truth. "Climb to the top of the mountain behind the castle. When you reach the summit, open the phial and cast the potion of truth into the wind. It will be blown throughout the kingdom and the spell of the wicked goblin will be broken."

To his great surprise, when the prince reached the summit of the mountain, he saw the white raven soaring high above him. As the prince opened the phial, the bird swooped down from the sky, snatched it from the prince's hand, and rose high on the wind, scattering the precious potion as it flew. Then the bird dropped to earth at the feet of the prince and before his eyes transformed into a beautiful princess—the loveliest woman the prince had ever seen.

As the drops of potion were spread through the sky, it was as if a dark cloud lifted from the land. All over the kingdom people suddenly felt transformed. They were no longer strangers to themselves. And the king realized that he no longer needed the magic mirror to know how to rule wisely and well.

Princess White Raven told the prince that when the potion of truth had lifted the curse that was on the kingdom, it had also broken the spell that the wicked goblin had put on her and enabled her to return to her true form. She and the prince were quickly married and in due course became king and queen and lived happily ever after.

"Know thyself"

Perhaps, as you read this fairy tale, you were casting people you know in particular roles and thinking of a very different stage for its action from the king's castle or the deep, dark wood. Does your organization most resemble the peaceful, productive kingdom with which the story begins? Or is it more like the chaotic, dysfunctional kingdom it descends into, where people begin to wonder what they are supposed to be doing and where the organization is heading? I hope for your sake you meet more white ravens than evil goblins.

I once worked with a family firm that had lost direction in a very similar way to the kingdom in this story. Voltaire said, "The human brain is a complex organ with the wonderful power of enabling man to find reasons for continuing to believe whatever it is that he wants to believe," and Gabriel, the CEO of the firm, exemplified Voltaire's observation. He was convinced that he was on the right track, whatever he did, and had an extraordinary ability to fool himself.

His propensity for self-delusion only became visible when Gabriel became CEO. He had been chosen for the job because of his expert knowledge of product design—an essential role in the company. Unfortunately, dealing with the day-to-day management of the firm was not one of Gabriel's strengths. But although his direct reports saw this weakness, Gabriel persisted in viewing himself as a highly effective executive. And indeed he did have some good ideas, but he was no good at presenting them in a cohesive, consistent manner. His rambling presentations led to considerable confusion. He set goals that suggested he was living in a parallel universe—his direct reports couldn't see how he could expect them to get from where they were to where he wanted them to be, but hadn't the courage to call him on the point. Besides, his total self-conviction suggested that their objections would get them nowhere.

Although the company was in a very profitable niche of the market, Gabriel's inconsistent, confusing leadership style began to take its toll in the form of declining market share and lower profitability. Everybody in the company knew that something needed to be done.

Finally, Evan, one of the more senior non-executive directors on the board—warned by some of the people in the company—realized that there was a problem and that Gabriel needed help. Having the trust of the major shareholders, he decided to try to bring Gabriel back to earth and help him acquire a greater sense of his real strengths and weaknesses. Luckily, Gabriel had always had a lot of respect for Evan. Over a series of discussions, Evan gently made the urgency of the situation clear to Gabriel. He told Gabriel he had to stop fooling himself and denying the reality of how the business was doing.

Although Gabriel didn't like the idea that people saw him as a fool, these conversations made him think. And this was where I came in, with a brief to carry out an organizational culture study, although Gabriel's covert agenda was to assess how the other people in the company perceived him. Unsurprisingly, everything I observed confirmed Evan's comments.

Subconsciously, Gabriel had known that something was not right. Painful as it was, he began to realize that his idea of himself as a strong-willed, capable leader had been simple self-deception—a defense mechanism that had been a survival aid growing up in his highly competitive family. His poor self-awareness had not only affected his own reality testing; more damagingly, he had externalized his problems on a much larger stage and the company and the people in it were being affected. He needed to sharpen his self-awareness, and fast.

This new understanding of himself opened up a whole world for Gabriel. Not long after, he hired a strong COO to help him with day-to-day business affairs. This modest reorganization allowed him to direct his energy toward the area he truly enjoyed: product development. The arrangement worked to everyone's satisfaction, benefiting the firm.

As the stories of Gabriel and the king in the fairy tale show, a degree of self-knowledge is the *sine qua non* for effective leadership. If you don't know yourself, how will you be able to know and influence others?

Embarking on an inner quest for self-knowledge isn't easy. It can be quite painful to look within ourselves and explore our faults, flaws, and the errors of our ways. But unless we take this step behind the scenes of our inner theater, we will never know our real potential; we will never know what we can or cannot do.

In the story of White Raven, the king knew that he could only be a wise, just king when he had enough self-knowledge to distinguish truth from falsehood and reality from illusion. Without self-knowledge, his sense of judgment would be impaired and he would be unable to set directions and determine priorities.

No other species except *Homo sapiens* seems to be equipped with a set of mechanisms for meaningful self-appraisal or to be curious about the whats and whys of our existence. To the best of our knowledge, no other species concerns itself with these existential questions. This human imperative to "know thyself" allows us to examine closely the processes by which we think, feel, behave, and act. It is the foundation of emotional intelligence, or the ability to understand ourselves and others. Self-knowledge is the most important element of wise, considerate, and effective leadership.

"Know thyself" was the inscription above the Temple of Apollo in ancient Delphi, and ever since the admonition to "know thyself" has been viewed as the quintessence of knowledge. As the king in this fairy tale realized, self-knowledge is the process through which we reconcile the glowing opinion we have of ourselves with the less flattering and even disturbing things other people think about us. Self-knowledge enables us to learn from our mistakes and keep on growing, developing, and changing. This makes introspection our greatest instrument for understanding what happens in our world.

Self-knowledge, however, is not easy. When Thales of Miletus, one of the original sages of ancient Greece, was asked what he considered the most difficult thing in the world, he replied, "To know thyself." We often resist knowing ourselves because we are afraid we may not like what we see. Another famous Greek, Socrates, believed that self-knowledge was important in order to find peace and happiness, and to become what we were meant to be in life. Plato, agreed, saying, "The essence of knowledge is self-knowledge," while Aristotle pronounced, "Knowing yourself is the beginning of all wisdom." They were articulating something that has been known since time immemorial. Centuries before, the Hindu Upanishads were asserting that "Enquiry into the truth of the Self is knowledge."

The search for self-knowledge is evident in Greek tragedy. In Sophocles' *Oedipus the King*, a series of tragic events unfolds whereby the protagonist gradually learns the horrible truth of his existence. What the play dramatizes is that Oedipus sees, but doesn't want to see; hears but doesn't want to hear. Oedipus cannot assimilate the truth of what he has done and who he really is: the murderer of his father and spouse of his own mother. When Oedipus finally attains the self-knowledge he has been searching for, he gouges out his eyes and gives up the throne. Following in Sophocles' steps, poets, writers, philosophers, and people in the helping professions have dedicated their lives to seeking out the elusive mysteries of the self.

Our inner theater

Penetrating our inner world doesn't come as naturally to us as understanding our outside world. Getting to know ourselves means discovering and getting to know everything about who we are and who we want to be. It is about taking a journey within, assessing what we like and dislike about ourselves. It implies acknowledging our strengths and weaknesses, our positive and darker sides. As the king in this fairy tale discovered to his chagrin, unless we know ourselves we will not succeed in even the most superficial tasks we set out to do. After the magic mirror broke into a million pieces, the king and his subjects could no longer make the right decisions. The loss of the mirror impaired their judgment. They were living in a world that had become distorted. Their contact with reality was broken, and they could no longer distinguish what was true and what was false.

Self-knowledge helps us to understand and accept who we are and why we do what we do. It helps us to act more authentically, something that will improve our sense of self-esteem, our ways of communicating, and the quality of our interpersonal relationships. The most successful leaders know themselves well. They know how to use their talent to the best of their ability; they have a good understanding of the people who work for them; they know their strengths and weaknesses and how to develop them; they know how they complement each other; they know the kind of culture their people will thrive in. They also recognize that no one is the worse for knowing the worst of him- or herself.

The fear of seeing things we don't like is the leading cause of our lack of self-awareness. Our resistance to acknowledging what we are all about is a real force in human behavior, as is the defense mechanism of denial. What if we don't like the person we discover behind the mask? What if it hurts to hear what others think about us? But while none of us likes discovering unpleasant things about ourselves, overdramatizing our mistakes and weaknesses will also hold us back from real personal growth. It is important for us to recognize the opportunities our failings offer us. When we discover that our behavior isn't working, we have a choice: do we work with what we have discovered, in order to change and improve? Or do we continue to see life through our distorted lenses, rationalize our behavior, and end up doing nothing or making the wrong decisions?

Understanding how others view us is a key element of self-knowledge, so we need to keep feedback channels open. A very simple matrix, well known in management literature as the Johari Window, demonstrates the challenge of achieving self-knowledge, dividing it into four distinct areas: public self, private self, blind spot, and unconscious.

	Known to others	Not known to others
Known to self	PUBLIC SELF	PRIVATE SELF
Not known to self	BLIND SPOT	UNCONSCIOUS

FIGURE 2.1 / The Johari Window matrix of self-knowledge

Discovering what happens in the great and glorious unconscious—the most impenetrable quadrant of our matrix—takes time and intensive self-analysis. The area where we can make the quickest inroads, however, is our blind spots (what is known to others but not to ourselves). Getting honest feedback about how we come across to others is one of the most straight-forward routes into expanding our self-knowledge, even if such feedback is sometimes difficult to digest. But the increase in self-knowledge may be well worth it.

Self-knowledge helps us to understand why people relate to us in certain ways. It gives us better judgment and the clarity to gain insight into why people behave the way they do—an essential element in being an effective leader. It also means arriving at a point where we can predict how we will act in specific situations, and knowing the effect that our actions will have on others. It also implies that we can be fairly sure of how others would describe our strengths and weaknesses. In other words, it implies authenticity in action—a key theme in the White Raven fairy tale.

Acquiring self-knowledge means a great deal more than simple navel-gazing. It also means doing something with the knowledge we acquire, changing our lives for the better, and living more meaningfully and pur-posefully. We saw in the fairy tale that when the fragments of the cursed mirror flew into people's eyes they became strangers to themselves. They lost their sense of who they were, and could no longer distinguish between reality and illusion. Of course, this situation is not without its advantages. There are always going to be people who prefer to remain ignorant of themselves, afraid that self-knowledge will be too painful, and cling on to their illusions.

Unless we can tolerate a degree of self-mortification, we will not be able to engage in full-fledged self-analysis. As we have seen in the tale of White Raven, there are evil goblins and other dangerous creatures to be discovered during our inner explorations. But to avoid the quest for fear of what we might find on our journey will only give these shadowy figures greater power.

The king knew (as did the wicked goblin) that without self-knowledge, without an understanding of the working and functions of his inner world, he would never be able to govern fairly and wisely. He would no longer recognize his limitations and would always be a slave to his impulses.

The tale tells us that effective leaders are eager to learn about their personal strengths and weaknesses, especially when it comes to dealing with other people. They are also quite knowledgeable about who they are and the person they can aspire to be. But the tale also tells us that it is not until we are lost that we make the effort to understand ourselves.

Mirroring

Humankind is one of the few species known to be able to recognize self in a reflective surface. For this reason, mirrors have always held extraordinary power over us, both literally and symbolically. Some ancient traditions saw mirrors as magic portals through which spirits left this world to cross into the next. Others believed that the mirror captured the soul when someone looked into it. No wonder that the superstition grew up that breaking a mirror would lead to seven years' bad luck. Mirrors have also acted as indicators of good and evil: the legend that demons, ghosts, and vampires have no reflections has endured throughout our history.

Magic mirrors play important roles in two well-known fairy tales. In Snow White, the wicked queen interrogates her mirror every morning for reassurance that she is the most beautiful woman in the land—until the day when she receives the wrong answer. In the tale of Beauty and the Beast, Beauty is allowed to see her father and her home in a mirror than hangs in the Beast's castle. In both these tales, the mirror acts as the interface between reality and illusion. This is dramatized in a different tradition, the story of Narcissus in Greek myth, when the beautiful young man's inability to distinguish between the two leads to his death. In the tale of White Raven, the magic mirror is a metaphor for self-knowledge.

Our development as individuals is closely linked to mirroring, in the sense of the way we use others as mirrors. In early infancy, the first mirror we see is the loving gaze of our mother. Through this mirroring process, we develop a sense of self and subjectivity and gradually close the gap between the imaginary and the real. And as we grow, we come across other mirrors—family members, teachers, friends, public figures we admire. Together, they mirror what we want to know about ourselves and the major themes of the cultures we live in. This kind of mirroring is central to our understanding of how we develop consciousness and a healthy sense of self. And it is a process that continues throughout our life.

The leader in the mirror

Many leaders underestimate the importance of self-knowledge and are not prepared to go off in search of this particular potion of truth. They go through each day reacting to events and getting by, rather than making conscious choices based on who they are and what they want. They are incapable of reflecting on their actions and motivation. Many simply don't allow themselves the time for introspection. It's true that the pace of life in the cyber age doesn't encourage time out for reflection, and too many of us go through life skimming the surface of who we really are.

The tale of White Raven shows us that acquiring self-knowledge is the most difficult task we all have to face, but, if we make the effort, we stand a good chance of achieving the happy ever after. And we do not have to make the journey on our own. The king and his sons had the help of a wise woman and a magic white raven, but our helpers are thankfully more down to earth. Leadership coaches and psychotherapists can provide the time, direction, and support needed to accompany our journey of self-exploration. They know what questions to ask and how to help us find the answers. They can help us identify our goals and set the waymarks we need to get there. What we learn about ourselves may not always be welcome. It's not easy to recall painful memories, confront our limitations, or make difficult decisions. Traumatic memories may even block our attempts at self-discovery, but healing is always possible. Without giving ourselves time for reflection, however, we will never learn how to make the most of our strengths or manage our weaknesses. Instead, we might end up living our lives on automatic pilot, reacting out of mere habit to the situations in which we find ourselves. We may resort to default ways of thinking that help us to preserve the status quo because that's where we feel most comfortable. If we resort to this way of behaving and acting, we need someone around us to point out that more of the same will only give us more of the same. Only when we examine and accept who we really are will we be content with what we have.

The price of envy

The second major theme in the tale of White Raven is envy. We see it in the wicked goblin's envy of the king's wisdom and popularity and the older prince's envy of his younger brother. Because envy is seen as shameful—a motivator that leaders usually do not dare acknowledge— we have devised myriad forms of self-deception to conceal it. But the competitive world of organizations, with their hierarchical cultures and reward structures, provides numerous opportunities for envy to flourish, albeit in disguise. Leaders need the self-knowledge to recognize when envy starts to raise its ugly head.

Envy takes two main forms: our envy of others and others' envy of us. In an organizational setting people may envy your position, while you may be envious of your boss, colleagues, or subordinates—there is no limit to the directions envy can take. Envy will influence the kinds of organizational decisions you make. While it may paralyze your decision-making capabilities on some occasions, it can be a strong motivator on others.

The philosopher Francis Bacon noted that "Envy never takes a holiday." Envy is part and parcel of the human experience and influences all our behavior and actions. In the same way, it is an unavoidable element of organizational life that needs to be taken into consideration when making predictions about human behavior. Including envy in the equation of organizational dynamics makes for a more realistic approach to organizational life. And envy isn't all bad. Having a certain amount of envy directed toward us is a sign that we have achieved something of value. It is also a motivational force.

Leaders need to remember that envy will appear in many guises (some constructive, some destructive) and be ever alert for the insidious excesses of envy-avoidant and envy-provoking behavior. A critical challenge will be to keep their own level of envy within acceptable boundaries. That's no easy task, because envy is quickly aroused and can easily get out of hand.

Sometimes envy is packaged (and successfully disguised) as moral indignation. We pretend to be very righteous about people we consider have transgressed some kind of moral code—for example, denouncing a colleague for living ostentatiously. This stance very often masks our desire to be in the transgressor's situation. When people obsess over someone's "despicable" behavior, they may well be masking their temptation to behave in much the same way. The target of their indignation may represent something they long for themselves. Again, a degree of self-knowledge will help neutralize the more harmful effects of envy.

The marvelous German word *Schadenfreude* means the pleasure we feel at the misfortunes of others. But if we base our happiness on enjoying the misery of others, what does that say about the overall quality of our life? Although *Schadenfreude* can bring moments of dubious delight, true happiness cannot coexist with feelings of envy, spite, and vindictiveness. Like the evil goblin and the prince in our tale, unremitting envy will inevitably bring us to a bad end.

The Spanish novelist Carlos Ruiz Zafón wrote, "Envy is the religion of the mediocre. It comforts them, it soothes their worries, and finally it rots their souls, allowing them to justify their meanness and their greed until they believe these to be virtues." Envy is a slow poison, as our tale showed, destroying our happiness and peace of mind. Insecure, envious people put others down to raise themselves up. They are unable to count their own blessings. On an individual level, a strong sense of reality and the capacity for empathy are the best antidote to the destructive effects of envy.

From an organizational perspective, certain preventive measures can be taken to mitigate envy. They include reducing hierarchical structures, engaging in participative management processes, eliminating highly visible executive perks, introducing profit-sharing plans and stock options on a large scale, and doing away with extreme differences in salary scales. Pre-empting structures, systems, and behavior that may induce envy will reduce tension throughout the organization.

The Self-Awareness Mirror Test

According to an Asian proverb, "He that will not reflect is a ruined man." This is the main cautionary message contained in this fairy tale. Without self-knowledge, we are sometimes as much strangers to ourselves as we are to others. At the same time, in learning to know other people, we become more intimately acquainted with ourselves. As this fairy tale illustrates, change and growth happen when we take risks and dare to experiment. What's more, self-knowledge is a continuing process—it is not marked by specific achievements and ends only with our own life.

The following questions measure the factors relating to your degree of self-awareness. Answer them stating *True* or *False*.

1. I strongly believe that if I want to improve, I need to know my strengths and weaknesses.
2. I believe I have a reasonable idea what I am all about.
3. I often question my reason for doing things.
4. I always welcome constructive feedback about my personality.
5. I can tell when people like what I am doing.
6. I welcome any opportunity to learn more about my strengths and weaknesses.
7. I always pay attention to the way I feel inside.
8. I make it a habit to analyze myself.
9. I have a good sense of my biases, preferences, and prejudices.
10. I am not the kind of person who speaks without thinking.
11. I find it easy to communicate with people who think differently from me.
12. I always listen very carefully to what others have to say.
13. I have a good sense of how to cope with ambiguous situations.

14. When required, I am prepared to share my feelings and beliefs with others.
15. I make it a practice to be self-reflective.

The more you answer *True* the higher your score.

If you score high (10 or over), you are the kind of person who spends a considerable amount of time on self-examination. If you score low (below 5), however, you may be reluctant to look inside yourself. Ask yourself whether you hesitate to monitor your feelings, thoughts, and motivations. If so, there may be a gap between your internal and external worlds, meaning that you say one thing but do another.

Self-awareness—the conscious knowledge of yourself—is the foundation of emotional intelligence. Self-awareness involves understanding your cognitive, physical, and emotional self. It enables you to manage your moods, behavior, and actions, and helps you monitor how you affect the people around you. Essentially, self-awareness is the capacity to recognize your own feelings, behaviors, and characteristics. If you have a healthy degree of self-awareness you are more prepared to admit your mistakes, welcome constructive feedback, and have confidence in yourself. Self-awareness also determines the ability to reinvent yourself—to learn to make more effective decisions, develop deeper relationships, and create greater self-fulfillment. But if executives in senior positions lack self-awareness, the whole organization is likely to be affected negatively, as this fairy tale has illustrated.

3

The Bear-King, or
The Price of Hubris

And on the pedestal these words appear:
"My name is Ozymandias, king of kings:
Look on my works, ye Mighty, and despair!"
Nothing beside remains.
Round the decay
Of that colossal wreck, boundless and bare
The lone and level sands stretch far away.
—Percy Bysshe Shelley, Ozymandias

Hubris is one of the great renewable resources.
—P. J. O'Rourke

We can never be gods, after all—but we can become something less than human with frightening ease.
—N. K. Jemisinok

Once upon a time, in the middle of a deep, dark forest in a land far, far away, stood the palace of a king who ruled over an immense empire. But although his kingdom was rich and powerful, all was not well. The people were not happy and laughter was never heard in the land.

The king was a cold, proud man. Although he had conquered all the neighboring countries, he was still dissatisfied. Instead of being kind, fair, and wise, he was cruel, arrogant, and arbitrary. Nobody lived up to his unrealistic expectations. However hard people worked and tried to please him, they were met with sarcasm and ridicule. If they made even the slightest mistake, the king's rage was devastating. He never forgave or forgot an error or a negative comment. Once, when one of his oldest and most loyal advisors warned him that the people were unhappy and suffering hardship, the king erupted in uncontrollable rage. "Get out of my sight!" he commanded his unfortunate victim. "If you enter my court again I will have your head!" As the old man left, the king turned to his attendants and said, "Follow him and see that he leaves with nothing but the clothes on his back. Seize his gold and his lands and burn down his house. He will learn what it means to cross the king."

After this, nobody dared bring the king any bad news. They made sure he only heard the things he wanted to hear. No matter what disasters befell parts of his empire, every day they would report, "All is well, everywhere." Terrified of provoking the king's anger and malice, they flattered and complimented him from dawn to dusk.

But of course, affairs in the kingdom were very far from well. While the king's self-importance increased daily, his tyrannical rule was taking its toll. The harvests failed, trade declined, and his people grew poor and hungry. But the king's counselors did not dare tell him the truth about his errors of judgment and the mistakes he made. Soon, the prosperous and powerful kingdom was full of misery and discontent, but the king, surrounded by flatterers in his sumptuous palace, saw none of it.

Many of the king's subjects decided to leave the country to find a better life elsewhere. Fishermen, farmers, masons, teachers, judges, and courtiers—everyone with a skill and a mind of their own settled in neighboring kingdoms that were ruled wisely and well. Those who were too fearful to leave and had to remain did so with a heavy heart.

When the king began to ask where his people had gone, his courtiers panicked. How could they tell him that the best and brightest in the land were leaving because of his cruelty and neglect? Instead, they told him,

"Sire, they have left the kingdom because they realized that they were not good enough to stay." And the king would reply, "Good riddance."

Eventually, as the power of the empire began to fall away, people in the conquered territories seized the chance to rebel. Worse, many of the generals and politicians who had fled the kingdom now helped lead these rebel lands. The king's rage when he saw this pushed him to extremes of vindictiveness. He condemned his truant generals to death and his subjects grew even more afraid of him. Their ruler had become a monster.

The king's courtiers now found that flattery and compliments were no longer enough to satisfy their ruler and began to despair. Then one of his attendants said, "Perhaps the king is lonely. Perhaps he needs a wife. A wife might help him to be more compassionate and merciful. If we hold a ball and invite the most beautiful women in the land, perhaps he will find a wife among them."

The courtiers were clever, and told the king that they wanted to organize a ball to celebrate his rule. The ball would show what a magnificent king he really was and make the rulers of the rebel kingdoms jealous. Pleased with this idea, the king gave them his blessing.

Despite the misery of their daily life, news of the ball lifted the spirits of many of the king's subjects. Such events had been few and far between. Everyone who counted for anything in the kingdom was sent an invitation, as were the nobility in the surrounding countries. The courtiers made sure that there would be hundreds of princesses, duchesses, marquises, viscountesses, baronesses, and noble ladies in attendance. Surely the king would fall for one of them? Surely there would be a woman among so many who could soften the king's heart?

The day of the ball came and everything was as grand, luxurious, and resplendent as can be imagined. But the king's reaction was very far from what his courtiers had hoped. None of the women he met was good enough for him; none of them was perfect; they all had at least one major fault. "She's ugly, she's fat, she's too thin, she's too tall, she's too short, her nose is crooked, her teeth stick out, she's too old, she's even older, she's wearing a wig, her feet are enormous. I deserve better than this."

One young woman in particular captivated everyone at the ball with her beauty and modesty. But the king seemed oblivious to her charms, even though it was clear to all the others that the young woman had very tender feelings for the king. When the courtiers introduced her, she shyly presented him with a gift—a cloak in a hundred different colors that she had woven herself. But the king merely said, "What use is this rag to me?" and rising to his feet, he tossed the beautiful cloak to one side and strode out of the room, out of the palace and into the wood beyond, snarling that none of the company was worth his attention.

In the cool of the forest that surrounded the palace, the king's rage began to subside. After wandering for some time he arrived at a deep, clear pool, fed by a spring and sparkling in the moonlight. Without a second's thought, the king threw off his clothes and slipped into the cooling water. But when he clambered out, quite refreshed, he found to his great irritation that his royal garments had disappeared. Furious, the king wondered who would dare steal his clothes. Who could have been so reckless? He would have his head for it! But meanwhile, what could he do? How could he return to the palace without any clothes?

While he was trying to work out what to do next, the king heard a rustle in the undergrowth and then ominous growling. There, making its way around the pool towards him, was an enormous bear. The ferocious animal was filthy, ragged, and starving, and had clearly decided that the king would be its next meal. The king had no weapon to defend himself and was filled with fear. He was going to die and be eaten by this repulsive animal. Would that really be his end? Here, where nobody would find him, rather than as he had always imagined, in state in his palace, surrounded by his loving followers and grieved by an entire empire? The idea was intolerable.

Just when all hope seemed to be lost, suddenly, out of nowhere, a stranger appeared. The king cried out to him, pleading, "Help me, please, save me!" The stranger called back, "I will help you, great king, but only if you grant me a wish." "Whatever you like!" screamed the king, who could feel the bear's hot breath on his face.

Immediately after he spoke, the stranger jumped before the bear, and with one sweep of his sword killed the beast. Then, ripping off the bear's mangy coat, he said to the king, "Great king, to cover your bare skin, I will give you another. This bearskin will be all your covering, your coat and blanket as well. My wish, having saved your life, is that you wear this bearskin from this day forth. Wherever you go, this new coat will go with you." And as he spoke, he threw the bearskin over the king's head and it stuck like glue to the king's body.

The king gave a great cry and tried to struggle out from under the dirty, smelly pelt. "Give me back my robes!" he demanded. But the stranger said, "Do not exhaust yourself. You will wear this coat until you learn what it truly means to be a king and how to rule so that your people are happy and prosperous." As the king stood and cursed him the stranger disappeared before his eyes.

Despite the stranger's words, the king continued to try to tear off the bearskin but it was hopeless. The skin fitted him as if it was his own. He ran towards the pool, thinking he might wash it off, but stopped when he saw his reflection in the water. Dark, dirty hair covered his face, his teeth were yellow and menacing, his eyes were small, black and mean-looking and his fingers ended in claws. He looked like a creature from a nightmare.

Nevertheless, the Bear-King decided to return to the palace. He was sure that, when he addressed his guards, they would recognize him and let him in. Then he would tell his greatest counselors to find a way to lift the stranger's curse.

But when the guards saw the strange creature approaching the palace gate, they threw sticks and stones at it to drive it away. When the Bear-King called out to them, saying "I am your king, let me into my palace," they fell about laughing, a sound that had not been heard in the kingdom for many years. "Why, your majesty," they mocked, "how delightful you look and how sweet you smell! This is certainly the way to find a wife! Now get along, you monster, and if you return we will kill you."

The Bear-King was outraged. How dare they laugh at him! How dare they make fun of him! How dare they say he was ugly and smelled! Did none of them have any pity for him in his present state?

Chased away by his guards, the king had no choice but to roam the land. But everywhere he went, the sight of him terrified the people he encountered. Just a short time before he had been the most feared and powerful person in the kingdom; now he was a monster, turned away from people's homes, threatened, and shunned. As he wandered from place to place, the Bear-King began to realize how much misery he had caused his people. Everywhere he went, he saw how little food and money they had and how suspicious they were of each other. And nobody had a good word for the king. In fact they blamed his arrogance and self-regard for all their troubles. "One monster in the kingdom is enough," they said, as they beat the Bear-King away from their villages.

"How selfish I have been!" thought the Bear-King now. "I believed everyone loved me, but they fear and despise me. There is no kindness and pity in my kingdom because I drove it out with my own cruelty. I ruled my people when I should have served them. I do not deserve any better than this." So it was that the king's old arrogance began to melt away and he grew humble, gentle, and kind. "When I looked like a king, I was a monster inside," sighed the Bear-King. "Now I have become a monster, but know what a king should be. How strange life is, when a curse becomes a blessing."

As time went on, the Bear-King grew used to his life as an outcast. He took work where he found it—often nasty, dirty work that no one else would do—and slept and sheltered where he could. Although his monstrous appearance did not change and some people still ran away from him in fear, others realized that he was no danger to them and he met many acts of kindness. When people were cruel and mocked him, he was reminded of his old ways and vowed never to be that king again. When people pitied him and gave him food and shelter, he vowed to be like them if he was ever free from the curse and became king again. When he had food and money to spare, he gave it to those who were worse off than himself, and with each gift he made a wish that his good actions might help lift the curse. He was no longer bitter about his strange fate. Instead he made the best of what he had and what he could do and was glad to feel strong and able to work hard to help other people.

One night, after he had been wandering for a very long time, the Bear-King took shelter in a cave. He was very hungry, as he had had nothing to eat for several days apart from roots and berries he gathered in the forest. In the cave he found a massive wooden chest, carved with an intricate design and thick with dust. When the Bear-King lifted the lid, a shower of gold and precious stones tumbled out. The Bear-King marveled at his good fortune. "I will return to the inn I passed on my way here," he told himself, "and buy a good dinner and a warm bed for the night."

But, as had happened so many times before, when the Bear-King knocked at the door of the inn, the innkeeper refused to let him in, as his appearance would frighten the other guests. However, when the Bear-King showed her some of his gold, the innkeeper's attitude softened. "You can sleep in the stable and I hope you won't frighten the horses," she said. But she made the Bear-King promise not let himself be seen by the other guests. "You may as well clean the stable, too," she added. "It's filthy and I can't get anyone to do the job." The Bear-King readily agreed to this, as he was used to doing the kind of work that nobody wanted.

By the time the innkeeper brought him his food, the Bear-King had cleared, swept, scrubbed, and polished the stable and strewn fresh, sweet straw to sleep on. But as he lay down to rest, he heard soft weeping outside the stable door. Quietly, he rose to see who was making the sound and saw an old man who was sobbing bitterly. Catching sight of the Bear-King, the old man gave a cry of fright and tried to run away. But the Bear-King spoke kindly to him and invited the old man into the warm, clean stable to rest and tell him the cause of all his grief.

The old man told the Bear-King that he was a nobleman who had fallen out of favor with the king. He had tried to warn the king that things were not going well in the kingdom—that people were poor and unhappy and planning to leave. But the king had not appreciated his honesty. He had thrown the old man out of the palace, confiscated all his belongings and burned down his house. Now the old man was reduced to begging for food and drink. "I am old and tired," sobbed the old man, "and cannot go on much longer. Then what will become of my three poor daughters? They will starve."

The Bear-King was full of sorrow when he realized that he had been the cause of all the old man's misery. "If this is your only problem, I can help you," he said. "I have money enough." And he put a bag of gold into the poor man's hand.

The old man was beside himself with happiness and gratitude and demanded that the Bear-King tell him what he could do for him in return. The Bear-King sighed. "I am very lonely," he said, "but look at me—who will want to give me their company?"

"I shall!" said the old man straight away. "You shall come and stay with me and my daughters. It is little more than a hovel, but we will make room for you. All of my daughters are very beautiful and you shall have your choice of them for your wife. When they hear how kind you have been to me, I am sure that one of them will agree to be your bride. You are not handsome, it's true, but it's what is in your heart that counts. I'm sure that my daughters will recognize how kind you are."

The Bear-King was overjoyed at the old man's words. Might he have a chance of happiness and a better life? He accepted the old man's offer and followed him to his lodging.

When the two arrived, the old man thought it wise to ask the Bear-King to wait outside while he told his daughters what he had promised. While the old man was explaining what had happened, the oldest girl looked through the window and saw the Bear-King. Screaming, she ran out and hid in the garden. The second daughter then looked through the window and said, "How can you suggest this monster could be a husband for me, father? He is far too ugly to have around every day. I will marry him over my dead body." With that, she slipped away and hid in the cellar.

However, his youngest daughter said, "Father, from all you have told us, this creature must have a very good heart. A good heart counts for more than good looks. I will be very happy to take him for my husband." With this she opened the door and asked the Bear-King to come inside.

When the Bear-King saw the young woman, he recognized her straight away. She was the girl who had offered him the beautiful cloak at the ball. He remembered that he had thrown it away and not even thanked her. Now he saw that she was beautiful as well as kind. How could he not have noticed this when he first met her? He considered how ugly, vile and dirty he now appeared. "Why doesn't she run away like the others?" he asked himself. "Why is she willing to accept me as her husband?" When the young woman approached him, smiling, and gave him a glass of wine, he could not help asking, "Why have you agreed to marry a monster like me?" The young woman replied, "I do not see a monster. I see the person who pitied and helped my father and his daughters. To me, you are the most lovable person in the world, and I will love you as much as I am able."

The Bear-King was deeply touched by her words. This lovely young woman was willing to love him for his character, not for his outward appearance. She saw past his ugly face and hideous, hairy body to the true, good heart within. But these happy thoughts quickly made him very sad. How could he ask this sweet girl to marry him while the stranger's curse lay upon him? Sighing, he told her: "I swear that you will be my bride, but I cannot marry you yet. I have to leave you now, but take this ring and keep it as a reminder of me. I have another just like it and I will look at it and shine it every day and remember you. When I am ready, I will return and we will be married." Then the Bear-King slipped the ring on her finger and said, "If I do not return, you are free of your bond to me, for if I do not return I fear I shall be dead." With this, the Bear-King went on his way.

The poor bride-to-be was very unhappy to see the Bear-King leave and her eyes filled with tears. Her sisters did nothing to comfort her. Indeed, they mocked and teased her. "How can you agree to marry such a monster? Nobody will believe that you love him. Everyone will laugh at you." But the youngest daughter did her best to ignore her unkind sisters and when she looked at the Bear-King's ring and shone the beautiful jewel that was set in it, she whispered a wish to herself, "Keep him safe until he returns to me."

By now, a year had passed since the stranger had saved the king's life in the forest and transformed him with the curse that had strangely proved a blessing. The Bear-King decided to return to the sparkling pool where his adventure had begun. Perhaps the stranger knew about his hard work and acts of charity and his fervent wishes for the spell to be broken. When the Bear-King arrived at the pool, he called out to the stranger, "Are you there? Here am I once more and greatly changed." There was a rush of wind and the stranger stood before him. "You look much the same to me," he said. "How is it that you are changed?" So the Bear-King said, "I have wandered through this kingdom and learned about pride and cruelty, poverty and hardship. I have learned about kindness and pity, charity and humility. Thanks to you, I have learned that a curse can prove to be a blessing and that a humble heart is worth more than a king's crown." As the Bear-King said these words, the spell was broken, the dirty bearskin fell from his body, and his royal robes reappeared by the side of the pool.

The king turned to thank the stranger once more but he had disappeared. Putting on his splendid clothes, the king set out for the palace. When he arrived at the gates, the same sentries were there who had thrown sticks and stones at him and driven him away. Seeing the king approach, they threw the gates open wide and cried, "Your majesty! You are safe! Did you not see the hideous beast that was just here? It claimed to be king and tried to enter the palace. We were afraid it had done you harm!" And so the king learned that the stranger's spell had made it seem that he had never been away.

The ball had finished, the noble guests had left and the palace was quiet. As the king made his way to his chamber, he noticed how people shrank from him and turned their heads away in fear, just as people had turned in terror from the Bear-King. His heart was heavy with remorse and shame; now he looked like a king but people saw him as a monster. "I will make amends," he swore to himself. "I will show my people that

I am properly humbled. I will show them that I have learned to love them and despise my former self."

The next day, the king took to his throne and called his four most loyal counselors to him. To each he gave a purse full of gold and told them, "Take this gold and go out into the kingdom, to the north, south, east, and west. Help the farmers to till the land and sow their crops. Help the masons to repair the bridges and the people's cottages. See that the drudges who clear, sweep, scrub, and polish have food and clothing and somewhere to sleep. Whenever you see a man or woman giving alms to a beggar, give that beggar five times what they give and tell them they have the blessing of their king. And if you come upon a poor creature who looks neither man nor beast and nothing so much as a monster, give it food and shelter because you will find it has a good heart."

The people were full of wonder. How their king had changed! Now he no longer scowled and raged and threatened. Now he smiled and asked his courtiers for advice and listened to what they said. Now he greeted his subjects when he passed them in the palace or rode through the streets. He stopped to admire and praise their work, their homes, their vegetable gardens, and their orchards. "Why, we thought he was a proud and heartless monster," the people said to each other. "But he has shown us that he has a warm and caring heart."

One day, seeing that matters of state were now in order, the king called for the royal carriage with its eight white horses to be brought to him and told his coachmen to drive to the old man's cottage. The old man began to tremble with fear when he saw his oppressor's carriage at his door, but he bravely invited the king to enter. Imagine his bewilderment when the king greeted him gently, asked after his health and for his permission to sit down, and praised the neatness and comfort of his home. The old man could barely stammer his gratitude for the king's comments, then asked what he could do for the king. To his amazement, the king asked to meet his three daughters. "I know that they are very beautiful," he said, "and I have determined that one of your daughters shall be my queen." The old man went swiftly to fetch them.

When the two oldest daughters heard who their visitor was and why he had come they pulled on their finest dresses and rushed to greet him. They elbowed and pinched and stamped on each other's feet in an effort to be the first to offer the king fine wine and delicious things to eat. The king thanked them politely, but barely noticed their smiles and simpering and attempts to flatter. He was looking for the youngest daughter, but she remained in the kitchen, in her shabbiest dress, longing for the Bear-King and full of fear that she would never see him again.

Finally, the king grew impatient and said, "Old man, where is your youngest daughter?" "Oh, sire," said the oldest sister, "you have no need to meet her. She does nothing but toil and mope and weep by the kitchen fire." "Worse," said the second sister, "she toils and mopes and weeps for a most hideous monster that she has sworn to love and marry." But the king would not be refused and commanded the old man to fetch his youngest daughter and bring her to him.

When she entered the room and saw the king, the youngest daughter curtsied deeply, not daring to look at him. She trembled because of her old dress and the smuts on her face, then trembled even more as the king reached out and took one of her careworn hands. Into her palm he dropped a golden ring, burnished bright with a sparkling jewel. It was the exact same ring that she wore on her finger and that the Bear-King had given her before he left! How had it come into the possession of the king? Torn between hope and fear, she gazed into the king's face.

"Yes," said the king, "I am the wretched monster that you promised to love and wed. A curse was put upon me because of my arrogance and cruelty and I roamed my kingdom as an outcast for a long while. But my curse became a blessing because I learned the value of humility, modesty, and a good heart. And when I had learned that lesson, I regained my human form and became a king once more."

With this, the king took the youngest daughter in his arms. When her sisters realized that the king they had just been flattering was the beast-like monster they had ridiculed, they ran out of the house in shame.

Who can doubt what happened next? The king married his queen; happiness, prosperity, and laughter spread throughout the land; and the people, like the king and queen themselves, lived happily ever after.

Hubris

Sadly, many companies are run the way the king ran his kingdom at the beginning of our story, and too many leaders show the same kind of arrogance and lack of sympathy for their people. As the tale of the Bear-King shows, in some cultures it is dangerous to speak truth to power. In these miserable and toxic environments those who dare to do so can find themselves out of a job, while those who do not dare become complicit with the dysfunctional regime. Meanwhile, those who can do so seize the opportunity to disembark from a sinking ship as rapidly as possible and find a more congenial billet elsewhere. The root cause of the derailment of leaders like the king in our story is hubris, which skews their perspective of themselves and their actions and those of everyone around them.

I once had a Bear-King as a client. Tom operated on the assumption that everyone should think like him, and that he was always right. He was a real know-all who could do no wrong. This might not have been such a problem if he'd been alone in the world, but he was running part of a large industrial firm and his behavior and actions were affecting thousands of people. Almost without exception, his arrogance, self-centeredness, conceit, boastfulness, snugness, swagger, and haughtiness were grinding everyone down. He expected everyone to be at his beck and call and make life easier for him. Some of those in the company who knew him better believed that he covered up his own insecurities by disparaging the people who worked for him. But whatever its origins, his behavior was causing serious organizational dysfunction and high employee turnover.

The longer Tom remained as CEO of the Asian region, the less people dared to disagree with him. They were all too aware of the consequences of giving opinions that differed from Tom's. His outbursts of rage were legendary. He would blow up about non-issues, even embarrassing his people in public. Although some of his direct reports tried to excuse him, saying that he only screamed at people he cared about, very few people bought that argument.

Tom never admitted to a mistake. Instead, he passed the blame for anything that went wrong to everyone else. It was very hard dealing with a person who made it clear that he knew everything about everything and that other people's opinions were worthless. It didn't help that whenever he was successful, he would hog all the credit, never acknowledging the contributions of others. He would publicly denigrate others' ideas, making them look bad, and riled everyone by telling them to be open-minded when their opinion didn't match his. No wonder that nobody who worked for him felt appreciated.

The only things Tom seemed to be interested in were money, power, and prestige. He loved being in the limelight. As time went on, Tom's tendency toward self-enhancement, accentuated by the adulation that came with his position, made him throw aside any inhibitions he may have had, making him increasingly difficult to deal with, and increasingly self-destructive.

Tom had been hard to take as a middle manager, but as regional CEO he became insufferable. The more successful he became in career terms, the more he appeared to lose his way. The fact that things were not going well in the Asia-Pacific office went unnoticed for a long time, as Tom was very effective at managing upwards—which explained why he had reached his present position. He was two-faced, appearing humble to his superiors, but totally ruthless to his subordinates. Most of the people who worked for him were seriously disgruntled and demotivated. Their poor morale was reflected in the company's declining results.

In the end, Tom's overconfidence set the scene for his comeuppance. First, the costs of refurbishing the regional office went way beyond the planned budget, a sign to the global head office that something was wrong. The tipping point, however, was a complaint filed to the global HR department by a number of executives at the regional office. Feeling they had nothing to lose, they summoned up the courage to record the negative effect that Tom's behavior was having, not only on the bottom line, but also on their emotional, physical, and mental health. Tom was fired at the same moment his wife decided to leave him, taking their children with her to her home country.

Not even Tom's sense of his self-importance could survive such a perfect storm of public humiliation and private misery. One of the few friends he had left knew me and suggested to Tom that consulting me might help him overcome his depression.

Although Tom did not receive feedback happily, I was able to help him realize the effect his behavior had had on others and how his arrogance had been an irritant to everybody, including his wife. After some time, Tom found a position in another company, where he realized the importance of establishing a new leadership brand. His was not an easy journey to improved self-knowledge, and he needed to unlearn many dysfunctional behavior patterns, but eventually he understood that the most reviled leaders are those who fail to acknowledge their own shortcomings.

Hubris—arrogance and unmodified pride in oneself and one's achievements—is a perennial theme in literary tragedy. Three of the greatest examples are Sophocles' *Oedipus Rex*, Shakespeare's *Othello*, and Milton's *Paradise Lost*. In that great poem, Satan determines that it's "better to reign in Hell than serve in Heaven." It is a tragic flaw that has also been dramatized on the real world stage in modern and recent history by figures like Adolf Hitler, Benito Mussolini, Saddam Hussein, and Muammar Gaddafi. Fictional and non-fictional figures alike, all came to pitiable and often terrible ends—but in this book we are dealing with fairy tales, which teach us that change and redemption are possible, so the story of the Bear-King ends on a very different note. The king in this fairy tale gets a second chance. Not only does he earn our pity, he learns to recognize his failings and make amends. So how can we achieve similar happy endings for hubristic leaders in real life? How we can help them retain a sense of humility and a sense of proportion in the larger scheme of things? Not to put too fine a point on it, leaders need help to stay sane, given the insanity of their position. Finding the right humility–hubris balance is a real challenge for people in leadership positions. When the balance tips toward hubris and too far away from humility, the problems that arise can impact an entire organization, society, or country.

As this fairy tale illustrates, an arrogant self has a voracious appetite. Presented with the loveliest women in several kingdoms, the king in our tale couldn't see a single one who was good enough for him. The more this kind of self-love is fed, the hungrier it gets, until it can never be satisfied. Ironically, the emptiest people are usually those who are most full of themselves. The ease with which leaders can fall victim to hubris necessitates perpetual vigilance. Because hubris bestows a false sense of invulnerability, it also leads to a kind of self-imprisonment, as truly hubristic people ignore every opportunity for moral counsel or shared judgment. It is very easy for people in positions of power to get to a place where they become completely blind to their own failings. Unfortunately, people suffering from hubris also tend to develop selective deafness. Never good listeners at the best of times, in the worst they only hear what they want to hear—and people who need to stay on the right side of them make sure they are only told what they want to hear. When they stop listening and participating in meaningful dialogue, leaders become the authors of their own doom.

Every day, the news media are full of new examples of the disastrous consequences of hubris. This dangerous mix of pride, ego, self-delusion, resistance to criticism, and (in the case of a company or institution) groupthink, can contribute to situations in which the protagonists are capable of making just about any mistake with the authority of "I know best."

Narcissism

Hubris is a form of excessively narcissistic behavior, something that is almost endemic in an organizational context, as today's "me generation" focuses increasingly on achieving personal gratification and self-fulfillment. To understand hubris we have to deconstruct narcissism. If we can make sense of the origins and destructive impact of narcissism, we may be able to find ways to curb the onset of hubris.

There is a healthy and unhealthy side to narcissism. Some self-love is essential for survival; if an organism doesn't look out for itself, it will die. On the other hand, too great a preoccupation with the self can be destructive. A certain dose of narcissism is necessary for us to maintain our self-esteem and develop a sense of identity. We need it to be able to form positive behavior patterns, such as assertiveness, confidence, and creativity. But, as with so much else, everything in moderation—and an overdose of narcissism can lead to egotism, self-centeredness, grandiosity, lack of empathy, exploitativeness, exaggerated self-love, and poor boundary management. If these darker elements of narcissism are not stopped in their tracks, the result is hubris, which, as we have seen, is seriously unmanageable.

So where do we draw the line between healthy self-esteem and a compensatory, inflated sense of self? This is never an easy call to make. As a general rule, though, we can differentiate between *more healthy* (constructive) and *less healthy* (reactive) narcissists. This assessment will be made on individuals' interpersonal skills, the degree to which they show a genuine interest in others' ideas and feelings, and their willingness to take personal responsibility for their behavior when things go wrong. It took the king in our fairy tale a considerable amount of time, pain, and physical and moral humiliation to achieve a healthy narcissistic state. Nevertheless, he did it—and the moral of the tale is that it can be done.

The essential characteristics of a narcissist are grandiosity, a constant search for admiration, and lack of empathy. Narcissists are flagrant attention-seekers who want glory, power, status, and prestige. Because they overvalue their personal worth, they believe they have an inalienable right to special treatment. Considering that rules are made for other people, they disregard the social conventions and are often arrogant and dismissive. They have very little aptitude for recognizing others' feelings or intentions that differ from their own—and even when they *do*, they assume their own wishes will take precedence over everyone else's. These behavioral traits alienate people who have to work or live with narcissists, as they do the courtiers and subjects of the king at the beginning of our tale.

We all show signs of narcissistic behavior, and in fact a modest dose of narcissism is necessary to function effectively. We can probably all think of people we would describe as serious narcissists, but who are nevertheless very talented and make great contributions to society. It is those who gravitate toward the extremes of narcissistic behavior—pomposity, arrogance, envy, rage, and spitefulness, like the king in our tale—who give narcissism its very bad name. If these people are leaders in the corporate world, they may engage in grandiose, unethical behavior, believing, for example, that obscene financial payouts and perks are their right.

Excessive narcissism develops in people who have been wounded in some way in the early developmental stages of their life. As a result of overstimulation, understimulation, or dysfunctional stimulation by their parents, they do not get the kind of attention they need for a smooth developmental trajectory. Phase-appropriate development is interrupted, frustrating experiences are handled badly, and parents are distant, cold, inconsistent, overindulgent, or too admiring. In this kind of unhealthy environment, children acquire a defective, rather than well integrated, sense of identity, and subsequently have difficulty maintaining a stable sense of self-esteem. They will also be more susceptible to hubris.

Individuals with this orientation frequently distort outside events to manage their anxiety and stave off a sense of loss or disappointment. To cope with these feelings, they create a self-image of "specialness." As adults, they continue to behave like attention-seeking children. Consciously or subconsciously, they have a strong need to be compensated for perceived wrongs that they experienced at earlier periods in their life. If they are belittled, maltreated, or exposed to hardships as children, as adults they will be determined to show everyone that they amount to something. If that determination stops at wanting—and working—to be valued, or extends to making reparation, excessive narcissism can bear healthy fruit. If it turns into envy, spite, greed, grandiosity, and vindictiveness, the fruit is can be very sour indeed.

What is the cut-off point between healthy and unhealthy narcissism? Unfortunately, determining that point is rarely easy, as it depends very much on circumstance. However, it is important to recognize when that line has been crossed, especially as we are highly unlikely to come across any effective leader or potential leader who does not have a degree of narcissism.

The self-confidence of narcissistic leaders can generate contagious excitement and have a very positive impact on organizational functioning. The considerable downside to this is that, more often than not, this sense of excitement is temporary and rapidly wears off. We meet the king in our tale when he is in the grip of excessive narcissism, but we understand that he may have been different in the past—energetic, astute, and inspirational. He has built a huge empire and his own kingdom is thriving, with a highly effective intellectual and practical infrastructure. But at some point the king has crossed the line. He has lost sight of his goals and now his vision is entirely self-directed. Over time, the actions of some narcissistically inclined leaders, which might originally have been seen as bold and imaginative, are gradually exposed as pure short-term opportunism. In extreme cases, leaders lose their willingness to exchange ideas, solve problems, listen to advice, accept criticism, and compromise. The organization slips into a downward spiral and hubris claims yet another victim.

A major challenge for all leaders is how to serve their people best. Leaders in the grip of excessive narcissism are unable to rise to that challenge. The main reason why they are so judgmental of others is that is a highly effective way of sustaining the fiction of their own perfection. They disregard their subordinates' legitimate dependency needs and instead take advantage of the loyalty of the people dependent on them. Like the king in this tale, they are callous, offering disparagement instead of support. Their behavior encourages submissiveness and passivity, stifling the critical functions and reality-testing skills of their people. Their lack of commitment, disregard for others, and narrow self-interest practically guarantee organizational self-destruction. The best people will leave and, like the Bear-King, they will end up surrounded by sycophants who tell them only what they want to hear and a cowed and impotent population.

Preventative measures

While it is difficult to demarcate exactly where narcissistic behavior becomes dangerous, it is possible to erect preemptive boundaries and design measures that can be taken once the problem surfaces. Too great a concentration of power—in organizations and society alike—almost inevitably leads to disaster. Most of us are familiar with Lord Acton's famous sentence, "Power tends to corrupt, and absolute power corrupts absolutely." Less well known is that he went on to state that "Great men are almost always bad men," a dismal idea that he corroborated with several examples of "the greatest names coupled with the greatest crimes."

Putting boundaries around leadership—introducing a system of checks-and-balances—is a corporate governance issue that entails clear and specific detailing of the role of the leader and other stakeholders in an organization. For example, in a business context, it will mean listing board responsibilities, defining the qualifications required to be a director, devising appropriate executive and director compensation mechanisms, introducing strict board performance-evaluation procedures, conducting healthy audit processes, improving the selection, education, and evaluation of board members, and well-thought-out leadership succession planning. Good corporate governance also has to take into consideration the needs of employees and shareholders, and must establish accountability systems that will encourage their participation in corporate decision-making. These measures will help balance the power equation. Restructuring roles will prevent the emergence of extreme oligarchic corporate structures, where leaders have complete control of the agenda.

This sounds great—and deceptively straightforward. But will attention to corporate governance principles be enough to prevent the emergence of hubris among leaders? We have to keep an eye on the person as well as structures and processes. How can we raise awareness of an individual's potential for destructive hubristic behavior?

To start with, it is helpful to know that latent hubristic tendencies (suppressed by young, high-potential executives or put on hold during the climb up the career ladder) are likely to blossom when people reach their ultimate goal of the corner office. At this point, any countervailing pressures from peers and superiors lose their power. For people at the top of organizations, predisposition and position often collude: power and excessive narcissism combine to make a monster out of someone who, until recently, may have seemed a reasonable human being—like the king at the start of our tale. Even healthy narcissists, having reached these heady heights, can go astray and regress, although reactive narcissists are more prone to succumb. Board members need to be continually on guard against the danger signs of this collusion and draw boundaries—dismissal being the ultimate sanction—when executive behavior warrants it.

Counseling and coaching by members of the board can often modify potentially destructive behavior. If that fails or if the board feels unequal to the task, another option may be to recommend professional outside help for the troubled executive. But while others may see that there is a problem, the leader is unlikely to do so. Only very few narcissistic leaders willingly accept professional help. Their reluctance to recognize personal imperfections and their tendency to blame others make them reluctant to expose their vulnerability and reach out.

When they do decide to look for professional help from a psychotherapist or coach, it's often their personal pain that drives them—feelings of dissatisfaction with life, futility, purposelessness, even fraudulence. They talk about the lack of meaningful relationships, dullness, and being bound by routines. They often experience mood swings and imaginary illnesses. More commonly, they are driven to seek help by a major life event, such as separation, divorce, or setbacks at work that precipitate a depressive episode. It is important that the executive and the board recognize what these complaints represent, because they are the cornerstones on which change effort can be built.

Working with hubristic leaders is never going to be easy: the coach or psychotherapist will have an uphill struggle. Narcissists are not inclined to acknowledge personal responsibility for their failures. It's all the fault of the "others," who are motivated by envy, set unrealistic goals, making even realistic goals unreachable, and otherwise put a spoke in the wheel. The sense of "specialness" and personal infallibility is not easy to change. Therapists and coaches also have to be wary of the narcissist's capacity to draw them into a collusive relationship and induct them into their mutual admiration society, stressing the stupidity of all non-members. They are very good at this and often succeed.

Constructive feedback, a key implement in the therapist's and coach's toolbox, is not going to work well with narcissists, who are hypersensitive to the slightest hint of criticism. A lot of time and effort will have to go into preparing the ground before constructive feedback will be tolerated. Bad timing will put a premature end to an intervention, effectively ruling out any further efforts to help initiate change, just as the king's treatment of his advisers in our story sealed the lips of everyone else around him. Narcissistic leaders will also need time to become more attuned to others and seek out cooperative forms of social behavior.

There are times during interventions with extremely narcissistic individuals when we might long for the ability to cast a magic spell or even for the presence of a very hungry bear. But accompanying clients on a transformational journey, like that of the Bear-King, can be intensely satisfying—as long as we keep a sharp eye out for the pitfalls. The key challenge is to enable them to recognize their own responsibility, regardless of the mess they find themselves in, and to make them aware of the primitive defensive processes in which they are engaged. Leaders suffering from hubris have to be weaned off their infantile fantasies of unlimited success and glory and helped to construct more realistic, attainable fantasies that will provide a healthy foundation for their self-esteem.

If we resist being drawn into collusion with the narcissist, and demonstrate an empathic understanding of the individual's fragile sense of self, the leader may eventually realize that something is wrong and take personal responsibility for it. Having done that groundwork, and established sufficient trust, the therapist or coach can then help expand the leader's capacity to consider others without fear of rejection and humiliation. This process will involve establishing a more secure sense of self-esteem, which in turn will increase the individual's potential for more personal intimacy, empathy, creativity, humor, and wisdom—the foundations for effective leadership. However, there is no quick fix for the trauma of having been deceived, exploited, or manipulated at a critical period of childhood development. Healing a narcissist is a lengthy and difficult process, as we saw in the tale of the Bear-King. If the process fails, others, as well the defeated narcissist, will pay the price in disillusionment and broken dreams. When the healthy pursuit of self-interest and self-realization turns into self-absorption, narcissists begin to view other people as mere means to fulfill their selfish needs and desires. Other people lose their intrinsic value and become commodities. But if narcissistic behavior can be bounded and made constructive it can be the motor that drives a success-ful organization.

The Hubris test

The following questions measure the factors relating to your degree of self-worth. Answer them with *Yes* or *No*.

1. Do you like to have authority over other people?
2. Are you concerned about form and image?
3. Do you have a natural talent for influencing people?
4. Are you easily bored?
5. Do you like to be the center of attention?
6. Do you feel you are special?
7. Is it important for you to get the respect you think you deserve?
8. Can you be a show-off?
9. Do you think you are more capable than most people?
10. Do you often believe that the rules don't apply to you?
11. Do you dislike being criticized?
12. When things go wrong, is it usually other people's fault?
13. Are you concerned about what others think of you?
14. Do you find it easy to read people?
15. Do you believe that you can be successful in anything you do?

The more often you answer *Yes*, the more likely you are to suffer from hubris. High scores (more than 10) may indicate that you are egotistical, self-focused, and even vain. You may be too absorbed with yourself.

Generally, hubris can create problems for yourself and others. If you can't empathize with the needs of others, but are mainly concerned with number one, conflict will be inevitable. Having a lot of self-confidence is not in itself a bad characteristic. The ambition to lead and serve for the benefit of the greater good can be an excellent quality to have. Too much self-confidence, however, leads to arrogance, the feeling of being exceptional, overestimation of the effect you have on others, and a sense of entitlement. Awareness of your susceptibility to hubris, however, will be a significant first step that will enable you to notice the signs in your behavior and fix this personality flaw.

4

chapter

The Kindly Crone, or How to Get the Best out of People

Motivation is the art of getting people to do what you want them to do because they want to do it.

—Dwight Eisenhower

Motivation is what gets you started. Habit is what keeps you going.

—Jim Ryun

Even if you fall on your face, you're still moving forward.

—Victor Kiam

Once upon a time, there was a woman who had two daughters. One daughter was very beautiful and industrious, but the other was ugly and very lazy. Yet of the two, the woman loved the ugly, lazy girl best, because she was her own daughter. The ugly, lazy daughter was treated like a princess, but the stepdaughter was made to work as a drudge in the house. No household task, big or small, that the stepdaughter completed was ever good enough. Her stepmother scolded and criticized. "Don't do it like that!" she would say. "Do it again, and this time do it properly!" Yet she never explained what the girl had done wrong or how she could do it better.

Life was very hard for the stepdaughter. She never had enough to eat and she had so many chores to do that she barely had time to sleep. While her sister was given the most delicious things on the table, the stepdaughter had to make do with leftovers. She had only rags to wear, while her sister wore the finest clothes made from the best fabrics that could be found. When her sister sat and showed off her finery in the parlor, the stepdaughter was banished to the kitchen. Her stepmother would say, "Who wants that bundle of rags in the parlor? Let her stay in the kitchen and do an honest day's work, dirty, lazy child."

The poor stepdaughter had to rise while it was still dark to carry the water from the well, collect firewood, light the stove, begin the cooking and do the washing. It was dark again before all her work was done. If that were not enough, her stepmother and stepsister would torment her all day, finding fault, inventing extra tasks and chivvying her to do everything faster. At night, she had no bed, but had to lie down by the fire among the ashes. Although her stepmother never thanked or praised her, the poor girl did everything as best she could, trying to please her stepmother and stepsister.

One day, when the fall had come, and there had been lots of rain, the woman told her stepdaughter to go out into the forest and collect wild mushrooms. She gave her careful instructions about which direction to take and threatened her with all kinds of punishment if she went the wrong way and failed to bring any mushrooms back with her. But in fact the stepmother had planned for her stepdaughter to get lost deep in the forest where there were wild animals that would tear her to pieces. "And not before time," the wicked woman said to herself. "It will be one less mouth to feed."

Following her stepmother's directions closely, the girl stepped into the forest, looking everywhere for the precious mushrooms. But she could not see a single one and all the time the path was taking her deeper and deeper into the gloomiest depths of the forest. The withered leaves crackled under her feet and the bare branches wound so thickly together that no sun penetrated to the forest floor. Soon, the girl realized that she was lost. It grew darker and darker, the wind rose with a sound like the howling of wolves, and a heavy rain began to fall, wetting her to the skin.

But still the poor girl went on, saying to herself, "I must find the wild mushrooms for Stepmother."

Eventually, she could walk no further and sank down on a log to rest. "What am I to do?" she wept. "How will I find my way home? And how can I return to Stepmother without any mushrooms? She will be so angry and cruel to me." As she wept, she caught sight of a little red snake that was struggling to free itself from a stone that had fallen on its tail. "Poor little snake, let me help you," the girl said. Quickly, she lifted the stone, and the snake slithered happily away.

Summoning all that remained of her strength, the girl set off again into the forest, still looking on all sides for the wild mushrooms. Suddenly, she heard a rustling sound in the leaves that were strewn around her. There was a small red turtle, lying on its back and struggling futilely to roll onto its legs. "Poor little turtle, let me help you," she said, and gave the turtle a firm push. Righted, the turtle waggled away merrily.

On she walked until, further ahead, the girl heard a bird singing so beautifully that her spirits were instantly lifted. Following the sound, she arrived at a clearing in the forest where a beautiful red bird was sitting on the branch of a tree, singing with all its heart. In her entire life, the girl had never heard such a beautiful sound. As she listened, the bird spread its wings and glided away. As if under a spell, the girl followed the bird even deeper into the forest. Just as she thought she could go no further, she saw lights glimmering in the darkness and to her great surprise, between the massive trunks of two trees she saw an entrance, lit by flaming torches, with a gate standing open. On it sat the beautiful red bird.

"Did you bring me here, Bird?" asked the girl. The bird merely cocked its head at her. I'm so tired, thought the girl. Perhaps here I will find somewhere to rest for a while. "Shall I go in, Bird?" she asked again, but again the bird just fixed her with a shining eye. "Well, I shall," said the girl stoutly. "I can always turn back if anything goes wrong." She passed through the gate and found herself in the large, beautifully decorated hall of a castle.

As she stood wondering where exactly she was and what to do next, she heard the sound of footsteps coming in her direction. Out of the shadows appeared an old, old woman with very thin legs, a big nose and sharp, metal teeth. The girl was terrified and turned to run away, but the crone called after her, "What are you afraid of, dear child? Stay with me. You must be hungry and tired. I will give you good food to eat and work to do. If you work well for me, I will see that you are not unhappy." The crone spoke so kindly, despite looking so frightening, that the girl thanked her and agreed to enter into her service.

The crone led the girl to a table spread with good things and told her to eat and drink to her heart's content. Then she said, "I have a large herd of cows and a very large barn to keep them safe from wolves and bears. But I no longer have the strength to bring the cows in for milking. Could you do this for me?"

Without any hesitation, the girl took a long stick and a milking stool, and went out to the meadow to fetch the cows in. And in no time, the barn was full of mooing cows and the sweet smell of fresh milk. The crone was overjoyed, and praised the girl for working so well.

When the milking was finished, the crone said, "I have promised the troll that lives in the middle of this forest some yarn to make blankets for the winter. Would you help me spin my yarn?" The girl was eager to show the kind old woman what she could do and in no time several large skeins of yarn lay at the crone's feet. Again, the crone was delighted and praised the girl for her work.

Then the crone said, "I have invited all the trolls in the forest for tea and promised them jam tarts, but I have no dough. Can you help me?" And in no time, the girl had rolled up her sleeves, measured, mixed, leveled, cut, and baked the dough and the kitchen was filled with the smell of warm jam tarts. Again, the crone marveled and praised her for her work.

From this time on, the girl took care to do everything that the crone asked, as the old woman treated her so kindly and looked after her so well. The crone never spoke angrily, even when she made a mistake, but showed her how things should be done. If things didn't work out as expected, she would explain how the girl could have done them differently. And every day, the crone gave the girl the most delicious things to eat and drink.

Soon the girl began to notice ways in which she could make the crone's castle even more comfortable. Without being asked, she beat and washed the carpets, sewed new curtains to keep the winter winds out, picked and preserved the late fruit from the orchard, fattened the geese ready for feast days, and prepared the vegetable plot for planting in the spring. And whenever the crone saw the girl going about these self-appointed tasks, she would thank, praise, and encourage her. And every time the crone praised and thanked her, the young woman resolved to do the best she could for her.

The young woman was very happy in the castle in the forest and stayed with the crone for a long time. But after a while she began to be troubled. She had not picked the wild mushrooms her stepmother had asked for. Her stepmother and stepsister must think that she was lost or worse, torn to pieces by bears or wolves. They would be angry and worried. Even though the girl was a thousand times happier with the crone than with her stepmother and stepsister, she felt that she had to return home.

When she said this to the crone, the old woman didn't seem surprised and replied, "I am very grateful for the way you have served me all this time, so well and so faithfully. You always give your best and everything you have done for me has made me very happy. And you have a heart of gold. Do you remember that on your way here you helped a snake and a turtle that were in trouble, even though you were in great trouble yourself? I know about these things—the red bird sang them to me.

"To reward you for all the good things you have done for me and others, I will give you this magic cloak and this magic bow. Every time you put your hand in a pocket of the cloak you will find what you deserve. Every time you aim this bow, its arrows will find their mark."

Then the crone took the girl by the hand to the castle entrance between the two tree trunks. The gate closed behind her and the girl immediately found herself back on the edge of the wood by her stepmother's house.

The girl put her left hand in the pocket of the cloak and pulled out a handful of fresh wild mushrooms. But when she put her right hand in the other pocket, she pulled it out full of gold. The same thing happened again and again. The girl realized that the crone had helped her to riches and freedom from the tyranny of her wicked stepmother. Stepping into the kitchen where she had spent so many miserable days and nights, she laid the mushrooms on the table and slipped away again without being seen.

The girl used her new fortune wisely. She helped so many people with her magical wealth that she became known far and wide. Even the king came to hear of her kindness, industry, and generosity, and so, of course, did her stepmother and stepsister. "There she is, helping all and sundry, and what has she done for us?" snapped the stepmother. "After everything I gave her—food for her greedy stomach and a roof over her ungrateful head. All she left us was a pile of mushrooms. I will bring her here and make her tell us all."

The stepmother was clever and sent the girl an affectionate message and gave her a warm welcome when she arrived. But after talking for a while, she could not help bursting out, "How is it possible that you are so rich? Tell me at once!"

When the stepmother heard the story of how the girl had found the castle in the forest and worked for the crone and been given the magic cloak and bow, she thought to herself, "Why shouldn't my real daughter have the same? Why shouldn't she go to live with the crone and become rich? Why should my stepdaughter have all this gold? It's not fair!"

The stepmother ordered her daughter to go into the forest and find the crone. "You needn't stay long," she said. "Just do what you're told for a while, then tell her you're sick for home and want to leave. She will give you the magic cloak and bow and then we will be as rich as your foolish sister." But her daughter was not easy to persuade. "I don't want to go and work for that witch and ruin my nice clothes milking cows and spinning thread and making tarts for horrid trolls," she said. But her mother nagged and bullied, and finally got her way.

With great reluctance, the lazy daughter entered the forest, grumbling all the while. Soon she came upon a little red snake that was caught beneath a rock. "Ugh!" exclaimed the stepsister. "How I hate snakes! I hope it hurries up and dies!" And she walked on, leaving the snake writhing in misery. Later she spied a little red turtle that lay helplessly on its back. The lazy daughter laughed as the poor creature waved its legs and rolled from side to side. "Good luck, you silly animal!" she called as she went on her way. But when she heard the red bird singing, she remembered to do as her sister had done and followed it to the magic gate that led to the castle.

Unlike her sister, the lazy daughter knew what to expect when the hideous crone appeared, and showed no sign of fear at the sight of her. She accepted the crone's offer of a place in her household and, like her sister, was given the task of bringing the cows in from the field and milking them. At first, she made an effort to exert herself, thinking about all the gold she would get in return, but she quickly gave up and the barn was full of the bellows of unhappy cows, desperate to be milked. "Dear madam," she said to the crone, "You must see that this is no job for me, with my leather slippers and silk gown. Perhaps you have another task that will suit me better?"

But when the crone asked the lazy daughter to help to spin the yarn for the goblin's blankets, she made a half-hearted attempt to turn the spindle and quickly gave up. "Alas, this is no job for me," she told the crone. "The yarn burns my fingers and my arms ache so much. Is there no other task I can do?"

So the crone took the lazy daughter to the kitchen and explained that dough was needed for the trolls' jam tarts. "My dear madam!" laughed the girl. "Eating pastry is one thing but making it? I'm afraid this is no job for me." The same thing happened with all the other tasks that the crone gave the lazy daughter to do and in the end the crone tired of the lazy daughter long before the girl herself was ready to ask to leave.

When the crone agreed that the lazy daughter could go back to her old world, the girl was delighted, and thought to herself, "Soon I will have the magic cloak and pockets full of gold."

The crone led the lazy daughter to the hidden gateway and, as the girl expected, handed her a cloak and bow, saying, "This is in return for your services. Both will give you what you deserve." The girl stepped through the gate and was overjoyed to find herself at home again. Eagerly, she thrust her hands into the pockets of the cloak, but when she pulled out her left hand it was full of dust and when she pulled out her right hand it was full of sand. The same thing happened again and again but still there was no gold. The lazy daughter shrieked with rage and bitterness.

Now, while the lazy daughter had been away with the crone a dragon had entered the kingdom and begun to roam the countryside, devouring the people's sheep and cattle and carrying children away in its claws to be eaten in its lair.

The people implored the king to help them but none of his counselors could tell him what needed to be done. Although many of his brave knights had tried to slay the dragon, they too had been carried away and eaten. The king sent his messengers out through the land to proclaim that the person who succeeded in killing the dragon would have anything in the kingdom that he or she wanted.

The stepmother had been furious that the magic cloak given to her favorite daughter had not made them rich, but now she saw another opportunity to obtain fame and riches—the lazy daughter still had the magic bow. Handing the girl a quiver of arrows, she pushed her out into the fields to await the dragon's next raid, saying, "I know this sort of magic—it works every time. Just loose the arrows and kill the dragon and the king will make us the richest people in the land."

Sure enough, the dragon swept down from its lair, hoping to grab its next meal. The lazy daughter took an arrow from the quiver, drew her bow, and aimed straight at the dragon. But to her dismay, instead of hitting the dragon, the arrow made a complete circle and landed with a thud in the turf at her feet! Again and again the desperate girl took an arrow, drew her bow and aimed but each time the arrow flew straight back to where she stood. The dragon, angered that someone was trying to harm it, flew down, grabbed the lazy daughter in its claws, and took her to its lair, ready for its next meal.

Overcome with anguish, the stepmother rushed to find her stepdaughter. "The dragon has taken your sister for its supper!" she cried. "Take the magic bow the crone gave you and go and save her."

Immediately the girl saddled her horse and rode into the wild mountains where the dragon had its lair. The ground before the entrance was littered with the bones and armor of its victims and in the middle lay the dragon, fast asleep. The girl gathered all her courage and crept past the snoring beast as quietly as she could. Deep in the cave, she could hear the desperate cries of her stepsister, whom the dragon had locked in a cage.

But the dragon was only pretending to be asleep and when it heard the girl approaching it gave a terrifying roar, flew up into the air, and prepared to pounce on the intruder and devour her. The girl took an arrow from the quiver she carried, drew the magic bow and aimed at the dragon. The arrow flew fast and true, straight into the dragon's heart and the beast tumbled to earth, stone dead. The girl ran to the cage and freed her stepsister, then taking the tip of the dragon's tail as proof it was dead, the sisters mounted the horse and returned to the kingdom.

There was joy throughout the land when the people saw the dragon's tail and realized that the terrifying monster was dead. The girl was brought before the king, who reminded her that he would reward her in any way she wanted. The young woman said quite simply, "Your majesty, I want to be your wife." And so it came about that she and the king were married, and a wedding feast was held, and they lived together happily ever after.

The motivation conundrum

I once knew a woman called Dorothy who had a gift for getting the worst out of people.

In her company, Dorothy was known as "the Stressometer" because of the negative energy she radiated and her knack for draining people of all enthusiasm. The process started the moment she walked through the office door. She ignored other people's greeting, brushed past them as quickly as she could, and never looked anyone in the eye.

Dorothy had so few people skills, it was a wonder how she got into a management position in the first place. She seemed to spend most of the day on the phone, with the door to her office closed. Although her name appeared on memos and emails, she was rarely seen. She didn't interact with people and made no effort to mentor junior colleagues. The only thing Dorothy contributed to the workplace was a negative social atmosphere.

Dorothy was an ineffective communicator who had a (conscious or unconscious) habit of withholding information, making it difficult for her people to make the right decisions. She was also unable to make decisions herself. If someone dared to ask a clarifying question about yet another incomprehensible problem she presented, she would respond with a snide remark about how she always had to repeat herself, sigh, or roll her eyes, making people feel they were wasting her time. Her lack of clarity was exacerbated by her inability to set standards: because she presented every task as a priority, most of the people she worked with eventually pre-sumed there were no priorities at all.

Also, Dorothy was emphatically not the right person to go to when looking for emotional support; she lacked the sensitivity, awareness, and listening skills needed to interact with others. Furthermore, she never thanked anyone for a job well done. Figuring out if she was satisfied was anybody's guess. None of her people felt valued.

Dorothy's colleagues took it for granted that she had terrible emotional problems and a miserable life outside work. Because she was so difficult to get along with, they all assumed she had no friendly or romantic relationships.

Eventually, they decided that while it would be hard to change her, they could at least make an effort to help her. What mattered was that they and the company should be successful; they didn't want to be victimized by her. They felt they had no choice but to compensate for her lack of leadership. They hoped that if they found ways to work with Dorothy's style, she would learn from their example.

They decided to make things easier for Dorothy. When a decision needed to be taken, they would present her with simple options. By creating the illusion that Dorothy was making the choice, they would make their own work in the company much easier. With luck, this strategy might help Dorothy learn how to manage more effectively. And surprisingly, their tactic paid off. Once the edginess was taken off Dorothy's behavior, she became less anxious and a much easier person to work with. Over time, she became a much more helpful person to deal with.

Motivating people to give their best to their job and the organization is one of the most important things that leaders can accomplish. Generally speaking, there are two kinds of forces that motivate people: internal (or intrinsic) and external (or extrinsic). Intrinsic motivators include the simple satisfaction of doing something we enjoy or seeing what we do as an opportunity to explore, learn, and self-actualize—in other words, doing something for its own sake. Extrinsic motivators are things like money, status, and fame. The main difference between these two types of motivation is that extrinsic motivation comes from outside the individual and intrinsic motivation from within.

Most leaders find it easier to deal with extrinsic motivators, mainly financial. Inside organizations, a lot of effort goes into trying to align individual economic interests with the organization's performance. Perks like onsite childcare, sport facilities, healthcare, and other benefits can also have a very positive motivational effect. However, the negative aspect of using these kinds of motivator is that they can have a discouraging effect on anyone who does not benefit from them.

This fairy tale is all about motivation and getting the best out of people. One of the two sisters excelled in performing the tasks the crone set out for her, while the other failed miserably. In the first instance, the proper developmental steps had been taken to enable the stepdaughter to give her best; in the second, all the crone's motivational efforts were in vain—the other daughter's previous history doomed her to failure.

Given the relatively circumscribed effect of extrinsic motivators (as we can see in this fairy tale), intrinsic motivators such as interesting work, psychological encouragement, or opportunities to learn become much more powerful than mere financial incentives. Leaders need to recognize that the carrot-and-stick method of motivation has only a limited impact. In fact, the diligent sister who worked for the crone had no idea that there were going to be material rewards at the end of her service. The second sister, despite knowing about the magic cloak, was unable to rise to the occasion. Her mother's developmental efforts had created a situation of trained incapability.

Getting the best out of people means knowing how to inspire them and helping them think outside the box. To do so, it is essential to create meaning—to appeal to their higher values. To get extraordinary results out of people, leaders need to remind them of the bigger picture—all of us like to see how our piece of the puzzle fits into the overall context. As the writer Antoine de Saint-Exupéry once put it, "If you want to build a ship, don't drum up the men to gather wood, divide the work and give orders. Instead, teach them to yearn for the vast and endless sea."

To make sure people buy into the bigger picture, leaders must also provide them with regular updates on what the organization is doing. This sort of organizational transparency is a key factor in getting the best out of people. And in her modest way, the crone in this story tried to do exactly that with the two young women who worked for her, while the wicked stepmother had not progressed beyond the carrot-and-stick method of motivation. Even so, the crone had no success with the lazy sister, whose habits were too ingrained to change.

Leaders have to be able to inspire people to stretch themselves and become better than they think they can be. This tale shows that the crone, in contrast to the wicked stepmother, knew how to get the best out of the stepdaughter. She motivated her to be the best she could be, and although the challenges she was given were extremely difficult, the young woman was grateful to be given the chance—and indeed after a time looked for ways in which she could do even more.

She had, after all, been exposed to a different mode of leadership while living with her stepmother, when she was never praised for work done well; indeed, it seemed nothing she did was ever good enough. What's more, she was never given an idea of how to do things better (not that doing better would have been acknowledged) and her demoralization was total. Dorothy's behavior had a similar effect on her people, and while she didn't go so far as to plot their downfall, her attitude drained them of all imagination and initiative so that their morale and performance faltered.

Leaders need to keep in mind that the people who work for them want to be recognized as individuals, shown appreciation, and given opportunities to grow and develop. Of course, it does help when a developmental foundation for the value of work has been established in an individual. While the lazy daughter had no idea of the value of work—even when working for such a talented coach as the crone—her diligent stepsister didn't need much encouragement to flourish, as she had internalized the value of hard work.

Developmental journeys

Leaders test their people and give them challenges to overcome. For example, in this fairy tale, the forest can be viewed as a symbolic assessment center, in which one of the candidates gains and the other loses. The forest stands for the unknown challenges we are all up against. In the world of fairy tales, these are bears, wolves, goblins, fairies, witches, trolls, or other magical beings that might waylay the traveler at any time. In our real-world personal and professional life the challenges are very different, but the unknown is still a place where we can lose and also find ourselves, like the two young women in the tale. The journey into the forest has the power to change lives and alter destinies.

The fairy tale also tells us that something important and beneficial can be gained from the interaction these young women have with the magical beings they encounter in the forest, if they respond to them in the right way. People on a quest (as budding leaders are) need sustenance or support, which these magical beings (like people assuming a mentoring or coaching role in an organization) can either provide or deny, contingent on the accomplishment of certain tasks. The crone in our tale made an excellent leadership coach for the stepdaughter; however, because this is a fairy tale, she could also be deceptive and whimsical in her treatment of her undeserving stepsister.

The novelist Mark Twain once remarked, "Keep away from people who try to belittle your ambitions. Small people always do that, but the really great make you feel that you, too, can become great." People achieve more when leaders set high performance expectations. Although these expectations are not always discussed openly, they can be communicated implicitly through word choice or behavior. But whether or not they are communicated openly, high performance expectations are critical for organizational success. Leaders who presume that their employees will shun work whenever they have the opportunity will try to direct and control them. The real test of leadership is to reframe what needs to be done in a positive, constructive manner and motivate the people who work for you in such a way that they are prepared to give their best effort. People resist being controlled, so the carrot-and-stick approach has only limited value.

When people are told what to do—when they are micromanaged—they cannot put their best effort and energy to the task, as they won't have adequate perspective on the implications of what they are asked to do. Giving people greater autonomy is far preferable to imposing a system of controls designed to force them to meet objectives they haven't bought into. Micromanagement is one of the quickest ways to breed resentment in the workplace, not least because it communicates a lack of trust.

People like to have voice in what they are doing. They don't like other people hanging over them. When leaders can let go—when they are not obsessed by control—they create an ambiance where their people will feel freer to make suggestions. This creates a corporate culture where people feel encouraged to present new ideas, which could improve the way the organization works. Involving people in decision-making processes will help identify potential leadership talent, which could help grow the organization in the future. And by delegating, leaders can concentrate on value-adding tasks.

The Pygmalion effect

There is a high degree of correlation between what we expect people to do and what they actually do. Believing the best of people usually brings out the best in them. This phenomenon has been described as the Pygmalion effect. But it cuts both ways. If leaders have low expectations of their people, they may inadvertently damage their performance. This phenomenon is known as the Golem effect.

The idea of the self-fulfilling prophecy is an important part of both these phenomena. People who believe that they are worthless or have negative perceptions of their abilities and qualities usually fail to achieve their true potential, and can confine themselves within self-imposed limitations. In contrast, people who have a positive self-image and believe they are capable of achieving anything they set out to achieve are likely to do so.

As a leader, it is important to create an organizational culture where, as Winston Churchill put it, "failure is not fatal." All of us make mistakes when learning and the only real failure is not to have tried. Anyone who has done anything significant has failed on the way. It is essential that leaders emphasize that it is possible for their people to fail forward and that failure will be forgiven—unless, of course, they make the same mistake over and over again. If that happens, something else is going on that urgently needs sorting.

Forgiveness is powerful. Truly transformational leaders are acutely aware of how costly it is to bear grudges, and how an unforgiving attitude prevents their people from moving forward. People who cannot forgive can get stuck in a downward spiral of negativity, taking everyone around them down with them in the process. Anger and resentment make us smaller, limited, and confined. Forgiveness is liberating and expansive. When we can forgive, we can move on.

The golden rule of leadership is to do unto others as you would have done unto you. This rule has remained valid down the centuries; its modern version is probably the exhortation to "walk the talk." Leaders need to set an example. If they don't walk the talk, they create confusion but if they lead by example they generate enthusiasm and inspire their people to work harder. Role modeling is easily overlooked, but is integral to people engagement.

Furthermore, when people do a good job it is essential to recognize and applaud their achievements. People like praise. Emotional stinginess is not a wise talent management strategy. People want to know that they are doing a good job and that they are valued. (Of course, this assumes that they are doing a good job—vain praise is not the way to go.) But if people are already doing a good job, encouragement can make them achieve wonders. Praise and encouragement are inexpensive and highly motivational. Recognition of past successes is a great motivator for future progress. And people appreciate positive recognition in any form.

Taking a genuine interest in the future path of a person's career will also have great motivational value. People like to feel that they are developing; they like learning new skills and gaining experience that will stand them in good stead in the future. Having these opportunities feeds their exploratory, motivational needs. An important part of motivation is support for professional development. When people begin to feel that they are stagnating in their current role, the likelihood that they will leave the organization increases—and employee turnover is very expensive.

Leaders will also do well to take a genuine interest in their people's work–life balance and give consideration to their family commitments. Their sensitivity to concerns outside the workplace will be greatly appreciated by the people who work for them.

Coaching for leadership

Coaching your people will always be a challenge. Some people—like the lazy daughter in the fairy tale—are hard nuts to crack. There is always someone who just doesn't "get it." No matter how they are guided, supported, and instructed on how to do something differently, they fall back into old familiar dysfunctional patterns of behavior. However, it isn't easy for most of us to change our habits. It takes frequent repetition before people can become comfortable with new ways of doing things, and they need support and encouragement when they go off track.

Leadership coaching can be a very powerful way to help executives become better at what they are doing. Coaching is not about telling people what to do or solving their problems for them. It is about asking them the right questions so that they can learn to do things for themselves. Asking questions guides people's thinking. Asking questions helps people change.

The tragedy in most people's lives is that they are far better than they imagine themselves to be and end up being much less than they could be. A good coach sees more talent and ability within the client than the client is aware of, and helps to bring it out.

Coaching people takes time but if it is done well, people will go to great lengths to solve the problems they encounter. The aim of a coach is to help people to see the talent they have within. As the German writer and statesman Goethe wrote, "Treat a man as he appears to be and you make him worse. But treat a man as if he already were what he potentially could be, and you make him what he should be."

The motivation test

The following questions measure how effective you are in getting the best out of people. Answer them with *Yes* or *No*.

1. Do you care very much about the welfare of other people?
2. Are you always prepared to praise the work of others?
3. Do you recognize potential in other people that they don't see themselves?
4. Are you good at challenging others when you think they are not giving their best?

5. Do you always try to get the best out of people?
6. Do you find it easy to work with people who are more capable than you are?
7. Do you always make an effort to make others feel valued for their ideas and contributions?
8. Are you prepared to give others tough but constructive feedback?
9. Do you like to help other people succeed?
10. Do you have the patience and perseverance to help people change?
11. Do you like to influence the actions of others?
12. When someone is upset, do you make an effort to understand the reasons?
13. Do you enjoy doing tasks that fulfill a greater purpose?
14. Does helping others energize you?
15. When you give people assignments, do you always consider their skills and interests?

Today, more than ever before, leaders have to win people's cooperation. The way to do so is through motivation and inspiration. The more you answer *Yes* to these questions, the more likely you are to have this ability. If you score low on this simple test, however, you need to work on your leadership skills and how to become the best you can be. You would do well to look for people who can help you develop the skills needed to get the best out of others.

5

The Four Brothers, or How to Build an Effective Team

Alone we can do so little, together we can do so much.

—Helen Keller

Talent wins games, but teamwork and intelligence wins championships.

—Michael Jordan

It takes two flints to make a fire.

—Louisa May Alcott

Once upon a time, there was a poor farmer and his wife. They tried their hardest to scratch a living from the land, which was full of thistles and rocks and had very thin, patchy soil. The weather was also unpredictable: sometimes it did not rain for months on end; sometimes it did not stop raining for weeks at a time. The farmer and his wife worked very hard, but they often went to bed hungry, so that their children had enough to eat.

The farmer and his wife had four sons. They all grew up to be clever, handsome, and healthy but they were all very different. The oldest son was quiet and studious. He watched the birds, animals, and insects at work and learned how the flowers, trees, and crops grew. He often pointed out to the others things that they had not noticed. The second son was very good with his hands. He could make tools and furniture, and mend anything that was broken. The third son was cheerful and very strong. He often saw ways he and his brothers could work together to help make the farm more productive. The youngest son was sharp-sighted and quick-thinking. He was a good hunter and often brought home meat to supplement the family's meager meals.

When the brothers were old enough to stand on their own two feet, their father said to them, "My sons, the time has come for you to leave us. You know that life on the farm is hard. The soil is thinner and poorer than ever, the yield is less every year and the cows are giving no milk. Your mother and I can no longer feed you all. Each of you, go and find a trade, so that you can make your own way in the world."

The four brothers were saddened by their father's words but they knew he was right. So, they took what few belongings they had, bade their parents farewell, and set out on their journey into the wide, wide world.

At first, all four brothers traveled together, across mountains and through valleys, until they reached a crossroads in a forest so dense and so dark that the sun could barely be seen through the leaves and branches. The brothers stopped and stared at the four different paths that led away in different directions, until the oldest said, "This is a sign that we must separate and follow whatever destiny has decided for us. But let us promise to return to this spot four years hence and see what we have become."

The brothers embraced, then each went on his way. Soon after he had set off on his path, the oldest brother met a stranger who stopped him and asked who he was and where he was going. The oldest brother replied, "I am the oldest of four and I am searching for what I can best be in the world." When he said this, the stranger replied, "Come with me and I will make you a glassworker. You will make lenses that will help you see the tiniest things on earth and the furthest objects in the sky. Nothing will ever be hidden from you." As he listened to the stranger, the oldest son realized that being a glassworker would suit him very well, and decided to follow him.

The second son's path took him to a village where he met a stranger who stopped him to ask who he was and where he was going. The second son replied, "I am the second of four and I am searching for what I can best be in the world." When he said this, the stranger replied, "Come with me and I will make you a blacksmith. It is hard work, but if you become my apprentice you will learn how to work any metal on Earth and make anything anybody wants or needs. I will teach you how to do beautiful and detailed work that will take people's breath away." As he listened to the stranger, the second son realized that being a blacksmith would suit him very well, and decided to follow him.

In his turn the third brother also met a stranger, a sooty, jolly person who blocked the path he was following. "Who are you and where are you going?" laughed the stranger. Like the others, the third brother replied, "I am the third of four and I am searching for what I can best be in the world." The stranger said, "Become a chimney sweep, like me! I am no ordinary chimney sweep. With me, you will scale greater heights than anybody else. You will climb and twist and leap and bound and the people who see you will be amazed and demand to learn how to do the same." As he listened, the third son realized that being a chimney sweep would suit him very well, and decided to follow him.

The path the youngest brother followed took him deep into the forest until he arrived at a sunlit glade where a stranger stood. This stranger asked the same question, to which he replied, "I am the youngest of four and I am searching for what I can best be in the world." "Come with me," said the stranger, "and I will teach you to be a huntsman. You will learn magical skills no other huntsman has ever learned. You will see birds and beasts no other huntsman has ever seen." As he listened, the youngest son realized that being a huntsman would suit him very well, and decided to follow him.

The four brothers each served four years as apprentices and did so well that their skills began to surpass those of their masters. When it was time for the oldest brother to leave, his master said, "I can teach you nothing more, but I can give you something to remember me by and help you as you make your way in the world. With these magic lenses, nothing will ever be hidden from you, wherever you go." And he gave the first brother a pair of binoculars with the finest lenses the young man had ever seen.

The second brother had become an astonishing blacksmith. He could make or repair any object under the sun, and not just in metal. As he prepared to leave, his master told him, "You are the best apprentice I have ever had. I have something to give you to remember me by and help you as you make your way in the world. With this magic hammer you will perform wonders with whatever you lay your hands on." And he gave the second brother a hammer that was as light as air but as solid as rock.

As for the third brother, after four years there was no height that he was unable to scale as nimbly as a mountain goat and as fearlessly as an eagle. "Now you can climb even higher and faster than me!" said his master. "Time you were off, my boy. I have something to give you to remember me by and help you make your way in the world." And taking his own boots off his feet, he said, "Take these magic boots. When you wear them you will be able to climb anywhere you want to go. You will never fall and nobody will be able to stop you or catch you."

After four years, the youngest brother had become a highly accomplished huntsman. When the time came for him to leave, his master handed him a magnificent gun and said, "With this magic gun no animal will be able to hide from you and there is no beast you need fear. Wherever you aim, this gun will find its mark. And while you bear this gun, whatever you set out to do, you will succeed in doing."

As luck would have it, the four brothers arrived at the same time at the crossroads where they had agreed to meet, embraced each other, and set off to return home. Their parents were delighted to see them all safe and sound and begged to hear the adventures they had had over the past four years. So the four brothers told them about the strangers they had met, and their curious apprenticeships, and the magic gifts each had been given on parting from their masters.

"Can this really be true?" said their father. "Let us see what you can do." Turning to the oldest brother, he said, "On that mountain yonder there will be a vulture sitting on a ledge. Can you see it?" The oldest son took out his magic binoculars and immediately located the bird. His father began to grow excited. "Is the bird is sitting on any eggs?" he asked. Again, his son raised his binoculars, and said, "It is sitting on three eggs." His father's eyes began to shine. "All my life I have heard that those eggs have magic powers. It is said that if you bury those eggs in the soil, the land will be fertile until the end of time. I know many farmers who have tried to get those eggs but none have succeeded. If anyone comes close to the cliff, the vulture pecks out their eyes."

"Leave this to me," said the youngest brother, and he took out his magic gun, aimed at the bird, and fired. Immediately, the vulture tumbled from the cliff. His father danced with happiness. "But how will we fetch the eggs?" he cried. "Nobody has ever been able to scale that cliff." Even as he was talking, the second brother had pulled out his magic hammer and begun to work. Within seconds he had fashioned an ingenious ladder from the bits and bobs that lay around him. Their father clapped his hands with delight. "But who will dare to climb that ladder?" he said. "Even if it holds, it will be impossible to reach the nest." "Nonsense!" laughed the third brother and pulling on his magic boots he scampered up the ladder, across the cliff face and onto the ledge where the vulture had made its nest, whistling all the time. Putting the eggs in his pocket, he leapt and swung back to the ground, where he handed the eggs, unbroken, to his father. His brothers cheered while the third son grinned and bowed and their father wept for joy.

"My boys," he said, "You spent your time well. You have each become the best you can be. You have learned to do great things and now you have shown that you can do even greater things together. I don't know whom to praise the most for getting me these eggs, so I thank and bless you all equally. May you continue to use what you have learned for the better of us all." The farmer buried the vulture's eggs in the poor, thin soil of his land and from that day forward everything he planted yielded such an abundance of good things that he was able to share them with all his neighbors and no one went hungry again.

Not long after the brothers returned, there was great unrest in the kingdom. A savage wild boar began to terrorize the country, tearing up crops and killing the farmers when they tried to protect their land. Whoever crossed the boar's path was ripped open by its great, curved tusks. No spear or bullet could penetrate the skin of the enormous beast. Worse, the boar seemed to have supernatural powers. The few hunters who managed to creep up to it unharmed said it disappeared before their eyes and certainly before they could raise their gun or bow. People began to say that the boar was a wicked sorcerer that took on a boar's shape to terrify the people or an evil spirit that could never be killed. The king became desperate for a champion who would help rid his kingdom of the beast and offered his only daughter in marriage to whoever was able to kill it.

Soon the four brothers heard about the king's great prize. "Surely," said the third brother, "if we put all our great skills together we will be able to find and kill this beast." So they set off once again until, after many days of travel, they arrived at the edge of the forest where the boar was said to be hiding. Yet the boar was nowhere to be seen. Now, all four brothers had learned to be patient during the four long years of their apprenticeships, but as the hours stretched into days and the boar still did not appear, they began to feel discouraged. Again, the third brother urged them on. "Don't be downhearted," he said. "I believe that together we will do what we set out to do. We will find and kill the boar and claim the king's reward."

Cheered by his words, the oldest brother raised the magic lenses to his eyes, saying, "I will try one more time to see if I can find the beast." Just as he spoke, he caught a movement and cried out to his brothers, "It is there! I have seen where it entered the forest!" and he began to lead his brothers in the right direction.

As night was falling, the four brothers set up camp close to the place where the beast had been seen to wait until daylight. While they waited, the second brother said, "No other bullet has been able to kill the beast. With my hammer I will make some magic bullets that I am sure will pierce its hide." And he set to work. As light broke, the third brother said, "I will climb to the top of the highest tree to see where the boar has its lair." And he sprang up into the treetops and was soon out of sight. When he returned only seconds later, he said, "I have seen the boar not far from here but it is lying in such thick undergrowth that it is unapproachable."

"Never fear," said the youngest brother, "while I bear this gun we cannot fail to find it and no animal I have hunted yet has got away from me." So saying, he took the magic bullets the second brother had made and followed the trail his brothers had found.

The youngest brother moved so silently that even the birds roosting in the trees didn't notice him passing. Eventually, he came to a gloomy hollow that led to the watering hole and lair of the savage beast. The youngest brother was so close that he could smell the boar and hear its heavy breathing. Slowly, he crawled closer and closer, until he was almost on top of the beast. When the boar saw the youngest brother, it rushed toward him with foaming jaw and whetted tusks, to kill him as it had done all the others. But the youngest brother shouldered his magnificent gun, pulled the trigger, and shot the boar through the heart. With a great bellow, the boar fell thrashing to the ground and for a while everything in the forest seemed to tremble. Then the beast was no more.

The second brother cut out the boar's enormous tusks to prove to the king that the boar was indeed dead. When the four brothers returned to the court with their trophies, there was great rejoicing.

But the king faced a dilemma. "My dear young men," he said. "I promised my daughter in marriage to the man who killed the boar. Which of you is most deserving of her?"

The four brothers stared at each other, dismayed. None of them spoke for a while, then finally the oldest brother said, "Without my magic lenses we would never have found the beast." The third brother said, "If I hadn't climbed the highest tree, we would never have found its lair. And without my encouragement, you might have given up our quest." The second brother said, "Only my magic bullets could penetrate the boar's hide." And the youngest brother said, "I tracked the boar to its lair and shot it through the heart. Only I killed the boar."

The king listened carefully to what they said and spent some time in deep thought. Then he turned to the youngest brother and said, "You tracked and killed the boar, but you could not have done so without your brothers' magic bullets, magic lenses, strength, and encouragement. None of you on his own could have killed the beast. It was only by working together that you were able to accomplish this great feat. Therefore, all of you have an equal claim to my daughter. However, she cannot be married to all of you, and that being so, none of you shall have her. Instead, I will give each of you a dukedom, with great, rich landholdings."

The four brothers saw the sense of what the king said. They moved to their dukedoms, where they continued to use their extraordinary skills for all who asked them for help, married four charming and deserving wives, and lived happily ever after.

Leadership is a team sport

Our fourth fairy tale illustrates the basic definition of a team: a collection of people with complementary skills and abilities who join together to collaborate. But what makes a team so different from a group? Briefly, teams have a high degree of interdependence that is geared toward the achievement of a common goal or completion of a task for which they hold one another mutually accountable. Teams reach consensus on common goals and approaches, rather than looking to a leader to define them. And the outcome of a team's activities will affect the whole team, not just individual team members. From an organizational perspective, team members are empowered to share responsibility for specific performance outcomes, and work together for a limited period of time.

The size of the most effective teams will range between four and 12 people. Larger teams require more structure and support, while smaller teams often have difficulty engaging in robust discussions when some of the members are absent. The team in our tale has only four members, with contrasting yet complementary skills. Broadly, one is a thinker, one a designer, one a motivator, and one a doer, and each is as valuable as the other when they are put to work together on the specific task of ridding the kingdom of a marauding wild beast.

Generally speaking, truly committed teams can accomplish much more than a number of individuals working on their own. By dividing responsibilities, different activities can proceed in parallel and the ultimate goal will be achieved much faster. As the saying goes, we may be able to hold a tune, but we cannot whistle a whole symphony by ourselves. High-performance organizations are the product of distributive, collective, and complementary leadership. This fairy tale shows that whatever the talents of one individual may be, no one has all the skills needed to do everything. Working as a team reduces the burden placed on any single individual.

While one individual tends to look at a problem from only one perspective, a team will supply multiple perspectives. Working as a team is often an opportunity to maximize each individual member's strengths and compensate for their weaknesses, enabling the team as a whole to arrive at top-quality results. One of a leader's most critical tasks is to recognize complementarity of talent in order to create effective executive teams.

I should add a caveat here. Although well-functioning teams are essential to the world of work, there are occasions when putting a team together to get something done may not be the best option. Some jobs or projects may be completed much more effectively if assigned to one individual. There are instances when teams soak up too much time and too many resources, flounder, and become a quicksand of tension and antagonism. Dysfunctional teamwork can be costly. But when jobs are very inter-dependent and tasks are highly complex—like the two tasks the four brothers faced in this fairy tale—teams can carry what may previously have been considered traditional, single-executive functions.

Complementarities

A group of carefully selected individuals can be put together in such a way that it becomes a highly effective team that delivers much more than the sum of its parts. The first step to putting such a team in place is to identify each member of the team's personality makeup and leadership style, and then to match strengths and competencies to particular roles and challenges. In this fairy tale we can clearly see how the four brothers made up such a complementary team. Each brother brought a specific skill to the task at hand. They all complemented each other to get the job done. The four brothers were the embodiment of the Japanese proverb, "None of us is as smart as all of us." The brothers believed that if one succeeded, they would all succeed; their reciprocity and interpersonal trust were a given. At both conscious and unconscious levels their behavior was in sync. They discovered that they could accomplish miracles as a team if they put their minds to it.

The attraction of teams

One moral of this fairy tale is that creating a winning team implies taking a collection of individuals with different personalities (perceptions, needs, attitudes, motivations, backgrounds, expertise, and expectations), and transforming them into an integrated, effective, holistic work unit. At times, this can be quite a challenge. Some personality types just do not click. A winning team needs complementarities, not incompatibilities. There is no point putting together people who are simply going to rub each other up the wrong way.

One way to approach this challenge is to focus not on what makes people different, but on what they have in common—the variables that make working in teams so attractive. In particular, teams can satisfy our need for belonging. In other words, while a team may initially be formed to fulfill a specific task, it may also meet other needs at an individual level. Many people like working in teams because they want a sense of social interaction, affiliation with a community, and the pride of accomplishment or greater purpose. Most people have a powerful desire to be part of a group in which they feel recognized and understood. And belonging—having a part in a social context—is essential for the development of self-esteem and self-confidence. In contrast, social outcasts may end up feeling empty and depressed.

Social connection (and fear of losing it) is crucial to the quality (in some cases, even the duration) of our lives. Applying this human characteristic to teams, individuals are likely to be less anxious about their work when they are part of a team that takes the time to build a sense of community and a sense of belonging for all its members. In fact, these intrinsic rewards may be even more important to individual members than financial or other more tangible compensations. Therefore, addressing each individual's needs may well contribute to motivating team membership and performance.

Altruism—the desire to make a difference—also draws people to teamwork. Many aspects of human social relations exist within a complex web of kin and reciprocal altruism. Working in teams that have a meaningful purpose—where meaning is created—may help people feel that their own ability to make a difference is magnified by the power of doing it together. The four brothers were not merely related; together they were also serving a greater cause.

To gauge whether a team is ready to deal with a problem, it can be helpful to ask some key questions. Do the members of the team have a shared sense of purpose? Do they all pull in the same direction at the same time? Is there complementarity in their skills and competencies? Is each member of the team pursuing the same thing? Have the team's goals and objectives been discussed and agreed openly? Does the team stick together through highs and lows, sharing both the blame and the rewards equally? Do they enjoy themselves most of the time? Ensuring satisfactory answers to these questions will help lay the groundwork for creating an effective team.

Follow the leader?

So far, so good. But outside the fairy tale, you are not really going to let your team loose in the organizational equivalent of the deep, dark forest without some sort of supervision. The interpersonal relationships that arise from team dynamics need to be managed in a strategic rather than opportunistic manner. This is easier said than done. Many things can go wrong when highly skilled individuals who have a realistic sense of their own worth work together. Something that always rises to the surface is which team member is going to take charge? Who will set the boundaries? Who is going to be the main action driver? And what will the decision-making procedure be?

It is always a risky strategy to allow the most forceful individuals to drive decisions about resources, as this creates a profound sense of unfairness and helplessness among the other members of the team. And group dynamics can become even more dysfunctional when the organization is in the throes of a succession process. In such instances, a zero-sum game mentality—"I win, you lose"—may dominate team dynamics, with each member of the team trying to position him- or herself for the top job. When "silverback gorilla behavior" is at work, functioning as an effective team will be difficult.

For all these reasons, a critical moment in team building comes as each member is integrated into the team. It should be made very clear what skills the new member has, and what contribution can be expected. Newcomers quickly, albeit instinctively, figure out how they fit within the team and the complementary roles they can play. At some level, their own individual hopes and wishes will also come into play as they join the team. The integration process can often turn out to be more difficult than foreseen. Leaders have to pay great attention to these kinds of dynamics in their teams. They may even have to resort to help from a professional team coach to have the team operate at its best. Team coaching can be a great way to deal with underlying team dynamics and to create a high-performance team.

I have pioneered this kind of approach throughout my professorial and coaching career. Here I record just one example of how coaching can help resolve the question of managing a high-performance team.

I was brought in to help Theo, the head of operations at his organization, whose management team was not doing well. In fact, when I first assessed it, I described it as a "pseudo-team." The team members didn't gel and there was a lot of tension in the group due to unspoken personal conflicts. I got the impression that most members of the team feared that their concerns would be too explosive if they were brought out into the open. Some team members dominated discussions and were regarded with open animosity by the non-participating members, who saw them as Theo's "favorites." Meetings were shambolic: team members came late and unprepared; information sharing was minimal; and people talked or whispered among themselves while others were speaking. The team was clearly not engaged and it was no surprise that it was working badly.

Most disturbing, however, was the team's complete lack of alignment. There was no clarity about goals and priorities, no evidence that members were committed to common objectives, and no sense that the team's objectives were meaningful to each individual member. The contributions made to meetings seemed way off the mark and little was done by anyone (including Theo) to keep everyone on track. The action steps that needed to be taken after each meeting were unclear, with no guidance about who was to do what and when; worse, some team members were unwilling to accept the decisions that were taken and sabotaged them. Any discussion about performance effectiveness was avoided. There was also a prevailing feeling among the members of the team that Theo rewarded people in a subjective and arbitrary way.

None of this was helped by the fact that team members never spent any time explicitly discussing group process. They never asked themselves how they could perform better and never considered whether the members of the team really complemented each other. The question whether the team as a whole had the necessary skills to perform the work that needed to be done—the question that clamored loudly in my mind—was undiscussable. Theo had paid little or no attention to assessing the talent within the team, and others in the organization were beginning to wonder whether he was capable of running it effectively.

After a number of missed deadlines that affected the rest of the organization, Theo got an earful from his CEO. Although he tried to make excuses, blaming others got him nowhere. His job was on the line. Theo realized that he needed help to be a good team leader and to learn how to build an effective team. My role was to facilitate the discussions that would have to be held.

Theo decided to organize a team-building session with my help. As an opener, each team member was asked to take a few minutes to rate (anonymously, on a scale from 1 to 10) how well the team was functioning presently and how they would like it to function in the future. When we looked at the results of the exercise, the gap was astounding. The next question everyone was asked was what they could do to narrow the gap between the current and the desired state.

During the discussions that followed, many suggestions were made about how to bridge the gap. These discussions gave each member the opportunity to understand better the concerns of other members of the team, as well as opportunities for them to support each other more and offer solutions to each other's challenges. The discussions also contributed to a greater respect for each other's differences and understanding of how they could complement each other, working with each other's strengths.

This initial session had two immediate effects. The first was that the atmosphere of the group became more informal and in subsequent meetings, they were more engaged, open, and comfortable. The second was that two members of the team decided that they didn't fit well in the team and left the company. With hindsight, the remaining team members realized that these two had been serious stress inducers and their departure added to the more relaxed atmosphere. Two new people were brought into the team, complementing the other members' skills.

This revitalized team became a real team. Guided by Theo, who now had a better sense of what his role as team leader would be, they became much more productive. They were aligned with what needed to be done and each team member's role was clearly defined. Also, a culture of accountability had been established. Milestones and target dates for completion were put into place. The open discussions continued to contribute to group commitment. Disagreements were no longer suppressed, overridden, or smoothed over. Conflict was viewed as natural, even helpful. The team members became much more conscious of their own way of working. Furthermore, they made it a habit to periodically stop to examine how well they were doing as a team.

A team's darker side

It's not unusual to see dysfunctional dynamics within teams where the stated goal is not the real goal, or goals are fuzzy, or priorities change rapidly. Theo's poorly performing team displayed some of the classic symptoms: role conflict and ambiguity; unresolved overt and covert conflicts; poor timekeeping; absenteeism; inability to achieve closure; rigid, ritualistic meetings; uneven participation; tunnel vision; indifference to the interests of the organization as a whole; and a lack of resources, skills, knowledge, and accountability. There is no genuine collegiality, collaboration, or coordination in dysfunctional teams. Unfortunately, this can give teamwork a bad reputation.

The effects of highly dysfunctional teams can be contagious; they have an insidious influence and will create a toxic environment within an organization. The competitive feelings among team members can result in sabotage of each other's work, unjustified criticism, and the withholding of information and resources, contributing to the breakdown of the team's proper functioning and the creation of a toxic organization. All these activities can be so subtle that the participants may not even be aware of what is going on.

Many dysfunctional teams resort to blaming and scapegoating, and are an impediment to an organization's productivity and the creative process. In these teams, members avoid dealing with conflict and discussions are likely to consist of generalities and platitudes. Unsurprisingly, many such teams morph into highly constipated, slow decision-making bodies, underperforming and floundering despite all the resources made available to them. Predictably, their decision outcomes will be sub-optimal.

Although there will be strong forces aiming at harmony and cooperation in most teams, the forces of polarization and regression will always be present, as will a regressive tendency toward "splitting." As humans, we have a tendency to regress and separate or "split" people into different categories, labeling the aspects of them that we find acceptable "good" and the things we find painful or unacceptable "bad." As a result (and because this is an interactive process), we may alternate between over-idealizing and devaluing individuals, teams, and organizations. Groupthink may raise its ugly head, resulting in poor, unrealistic, and even unethical decision-making.

While personality conflicts are very troublesome, structural organizational design errors can bring additional misery. Essentially, if good people are put into bad systems, we should not be surprised by their poor results. If teams are created merely as a gesture that some form of action needs to be taken, without giving the members of the team a clear mandate for what needs to be done (in contrast to the tasks allocated to the four brothers in this fairy tale), form will take precedence over substance, and empty rhetoric over real work.

Senior executives can also play a highly dysfunctional role by putting people into teams for purely political reasons—creating teams in name only. The members of such teams end up engaging in social rituals, merely playing roles in each other's presence. This behavior prevents team members from knowing each other on a deeper level. Recognizing the futility of their activities, they may resent the time they spend with the team. They may feel—rightly—that they have better things to do. So they go through the motions, feeling increasingly alienated from the organization's overall mission. In fact, the permutations of team dysfunctionality are endless.

All of us, at one time, have been members of a team; all of us have had the opportunity to observe that teams can evoke strong and often conflicting reactions. Moreover, many of us have learned from personal experience that being part of a team can be either highly attractive or repellent, extremely satisfying or deeply disappointing, depending on how well the team is functioning. Many of us know first-hand that a great deal of the energy generated and dispensed within a team revolves around frustration, tension, and ambivalence. Thus, given the importance of the emotional dimension of teamwork, people prepared to be team players have to focus not only on the tasks that need to be done, but also on the processes that make them possible. This is where team coaching can play a very helpful role.

Team coaching

Power dynamics are part and parcel of the functioning of teams. Many of the individuals who are part of a team are typically stars in their own fields. They may have been rewarded for outstanding individual contributions. Seldom, however, have they been rewarded in any substantial way for their contributions to the success of others. Some of them may have an excess of overconfidence about their abilities coupled with poorly managed anxiety about how to deal with each other and the challenges they face jointly. But when competitive feelings dominate, and people approach a team with a win–lose attitude, personal motives will rule while the interests of the organization become secondary. There will be tension between the cooperation needed to work as a team and the implicit competition of people who are out for themselves. As I indicated earlier, the stakes will be particularly high when these dynamics apply to a CEO succession race.

Frequently, the biggest difficulty in a team setting that each member has to manage is the ability to play multiple roles simultaneously. And some of these roles have built-in conflicts. For example, each head of a function is expected to maximize the effectiveness of that function. At the same time, the organization's strategy requires that resources (money, time, attention, promotion, etc.) be allocated in a way that maximizes the benefit to the organization as a whole. To be a constructive organizational participant requires some functions or divisions to control their self-interest for a time for the benefit of the whole organization. But it is not easy to prevent the silo mentality and turf fights that may ensue.

Given the presence of these power dynamics, leaders struggle with the problem of getting things done. They know that to create a high-performance organization they need to get everyone, from top to bottom, on board to execute decisions effectively, but they don't know how to really go about it. They don't know how to achieve matrix-like alignment for strategy execution. Instead, particularly in situations of highly complex organizational structures, they often find themselves in situations whereby implementation is stalled.

Without the presence of a team culture, executives may do things their own way, often resulting in uncoordinated, even conflicting, decisions and actions. A major leadership challenge is to stop such dysfunctional behavior. This is where team coaching can make a difference by ensuring that everyone within the organization can see and internalize the direction for the business and know how their job fits in within the big picture. The creation of a clear roadmap through team coaching will positively affect a company's success in execution.

Execution

When engaging in a team coaching effort, it is important to recognize that full engagement will not occur unless each member of the team can trust that the conversation will not harm their objectives or their future prospects. The mandate of the team coaches will be to bring the various factions that make up the team together in order to harness the collective wisdom of the group. Their challenge is to change the existing team dynamics for the better, paying attention to the individual personalities that make up the team. To foster this process, effective team coaches can help the members of the team take control of their key team functions: setting direction, creating alignment throughout the organization, and building the commitment of everyone needed to accomplish certain organizational objectives.

Apart from providing focus and addressing out-of-awareness behavior, team coaching also provides other substantial benefits. An obvious one is economies of scale, in maximizing the value of time and resources by bringing a number of people together. This is a more efficient way of doing things than one-on-one coaching. In addition, team coaching may contribute to better knowledge of different areas of the business through the sharing of real experiences. This will be conducive to a deepened awareness of shared situations, and help prevent a silo mentality developing. The buy-in of the various members of the team can also result in increased productivity through shared practices and lessons learned. Team coaching helps the members of the team acquire a sense of community. A synergy of energy, commitment, and excitement may be created due to the intensity of the process.

Team coaching interventions create an opportunity to receive coaching while benefiting from the successes and challenges of the other participants in the team. Through team coaching each member of the team will have a stake in the other team members' success. Although each member of the team often knows what they need to work on, a discussion of the issue provides greater clarity; it may create the kind of momentum needed to arrive at effective execution of decisions.

"Undiscussables"

Frequently, the members of a leadership team do not have a forum to talk about the challenges they face and how they feel about them. It is difficult to establish a climate that encourages adequate transparency, given the competitiveness between team members. The pressure to avoid addressing these issues is particularly significant in senior leadership teams. Encouraged by a supportive group coach, these and other "undiscussables" become more discussable.

Some overt or covert "undiscussables" originate within the team as a whole or within specific individuals. For example, there may be a poor person–job fit—the person just doesn't have the competencies to do a designated job well. However, none of the other team members is likely to want to be the person to reveal this elephant in the room. In this sort of situation, the team coach can point out that team members are engaged in "groupthink," and that faulty decision-making is taking place. Group pressures may have led to a deterioration in reality testing, a failure to assess risks, and even the dismissal of ethical concerns. Teams affected by groupthink often ignore alternatives and may resort to irrational actions. A team becomes especially susceptible to groupthink when its members have similar backgrounds.

There can also be systemic problems if the organizational architecture doesn't help the members in the team function well. The team coach's role will be to identify many of these "undiscussables," acknowledge them, and bring them out into the open. This is a highly effective method for showing teams how to reduce conflict and improve their working relationships.

Only when these "undiscussables" are dealt with can the team focus on its real work and achieve its objectives.

A willingness to be vulnerable

Team coaches play a very complex role. They have to maintain their neutrality as a confidant for all the members of the team. They need to be a container for the group's heightened feelings but at the same time be able to give challenging feedback. They have to develop an action plan for each individual team member, while encouraging the team as a whole to think more broadly—and keeping the broader interest of the organization in mind.

One of the major issues the team coach will have to help members confront is the general human unwillingness to reveal our vulnerabilities. Everyone dreads being regarded as a fool. Fear of self-disclosure may be associated with painful memories of childhood situations where we were exposed to public ridicule and humiliation. There will always be limits to self-disclosure. Teams in organizations are quite different from therapy groups, which have their own boundaries. Too much self-disclosure may leave team members with highly ambivalent feelings, creating an increasing sense of vulnerability. All this means that trust among team members is critical, and equally critical is the example set by the team leader.

When the leader is willing to admit mistakes and weaknesses, and express concerns, everybody wins. As members of a team get to know their colleagues better, they will come to understand the things that will and will not work for different people. For example, if team members know that one of their colleagues has problems with closeness, they will understand why that person prefers to work independently, rather than assuming that he or she is simply not interested in working with others.

Team, team, team

Team dynamics can take on a life of their own, influencing participants in significant ways. Leaders need not only to focus on the team's primary tasks, but also to make specific team dynamics more overt so that tasks are not derailed by unconscious acting out. In the best teams, members are ready to take personal risks, prepared to tackle conflict, and willing to have courageous conversations. All this, however, is contingent upon an underlying team culture of trust, reciprocity, and constructive conflict resolution. When team members develop an understanding of each other's strengths and weaknesses (as we saw in the fairy tale), they lay the foundations for a high-performance organization. The attitude and mood of a successful team can energize an entire organization, creating a greater sense of satisfaction, establishing a learning, collaborative culture, and contributing to a high degree of creativity and innovation. In organizations with an effective team culture, information flows more freely—up, down, and laterally—throughout the organization.

Life as a whole is a team effort. As the fairy tale illustrates, we can't all be good at everything. This is partly the logic behind having a team in the first place, creating a situation in which each role is filled by the person best suited to it and together every job and every strength is covered. To quote Albert Einstein, "Nothing truly valuable can be achieved except by the unselfish cooperation of many individuals."

Teambuilding test

The following questions measure how effective you are in running a team. Answer them with *Yes* or *No*.

1. Do you create clarity about your team's goals and values?
2. Do you make sure that your team is result oriented?
3. Are you confident that all team members know their roles?
4. Do you make an effort to create mutual trust among the members of your team?
5. Do you help your team members spend time building credibility with other parts of the organization?
6. Do you create complementarity of roles among the members of your team?

7. Have you created an atmosphere in which there is mutual support and assistance between all the members of your team?

8. Do you make sure that all your team members have voice and can speak their mind?

9. Do you make an effort to create accountability in words and actions among all the members of your team?

10. As the leader of your team, do you pay attention to both the process and content of team discussions?

11. Do you engage in constructive problem solving and conflict resolution?

12. Have you created clear measures of success for your team?

13. Have you created a team that respects rules, mutual commitments, and deadlines?

14. Do you encourage the members of your team to come up with innovative solutions?

15. Do the members of your team give each other constructive feedback?

The more you answer *Yes*, the higher your score. If you score high, you are the kind of person who spends a lot of time making sure your team is performing well. You know that effective teams can make a huge contribution to the success of an organization. If you score low, you need to make a greater effort to create an effective team out of the people you work with. It is important to remember that merely putting a group of individuals together does not make a team. A *sine qua non* is to pay attention to people's personal skills and complementarities.

6

King Lion, or How to Build an Effective Organization

There is a famous Sufi story about the legendary figure Nasrudin.

Once upon a time, an eager student visited him and said,

"Great sage, I must ask you a very important question, the answer to which we all desire. What is the secret to attaining happiness?"

Nasrudin thought for a time and then responded,

"The secret of happiness is to make the right decisions."

"Oh!" said the student, "But how do we know to make the right decisions?"

"From experience," answered Nasrudin.

"Yes, but how do we get that experience?" asked the student.

"By making the wrong decisions," said Nasrudin.

Once upon a time, in a land far, far away, there was a forest where no human being had ever set foot, and where there were only animals. Although the animals lived together harmoniously, the forest was a scene of chaos. Fruit and vegetables were harvested too early or too late. Rocks and logs clogged the rivers, choking the fish. Trees fell down without warning, endangering the lives of birds and animals. The time had come, many of the animals thought, to choose a ruler who would establish order in the forest and lead the animal kingdom. But who would be best for the job? All the animals had different ideas and many thought they would make the best candidate. The arguments rolled on and on until the screeching, chattering, roaring, and whistling became a cacophony of noise that filled the forest.

Eventually, the porcupine rattled his quills until he had silence and said, "Let's hold a competition. Any animal that thinks it would be a good ruler should give a short speech explaining why it should be chosen. After the speeches, we will have a vote and the animal with the most votes will be crowned ruler of the forest."

All the animals thought this was an excellent idea and those that wanted to be chosen began to think long and hard about what they could say to convince the others.

When the time for the competition had arrived, the bear was the first to step forward. "There is no question that I should be king. I am big, I am strong, I have magnificent jaws, I can climb trees, I can dig holes in the earth and I can swim. Because I can do all these things, I am the obvious choice." But the other animals murmured among themselves, "Yes, he can do all these things—but he is not very clever."

Now it was the turn of the giraffe, who said, "I am the tallest. No animal has a neck and legs as long as mine. I have a tongue longer than any of you. I can reach the leaves on the highest trees. Clearly, I should be queen." But the other animals said to each other, "All she's got is a neck and legs—we need more than that."

The elephant was next in line. He said, "I am the biggest, heaviest, and noisiest of you all. I have beautiful ivory tusks, I can push down trees, and I can tear down branches. Wherever I go, the earth trembles. You should choose me as your king." This time the murmuring among the other animals was kinder. "He's not just big," they said. "He has a brain as well."

But as their voices rose approvingly, the lion muscled his way forward and the animals grew quiet. "Enough of this nonsense," said the lion. "You have all watched me hunt. You have all seen my teeth and my claws and heard me roar. I am the most magnificent animal in the forest. I am already the king of beasts. Who else can you choose as your ruler?"

After the lion had spoken, there was a long silence before the animals began to speak again. Some said, "Lions are killers. He might eat us, not lead us." Some said, "He is very fond of the sound of his own voice. He won't listen to any of us." But most said, "I don't want to find myself at the wrong end of those teeth and claws," and out of fear the animals cast their vote for the lion and he became king of the forest.

If any of the animals had hoped that the lion would prove to be a good leader, they were mistaken. Nothing changed in the forest. The crops continued to fail, the rivers remained blocked, and trees fell faster than ever. Worse, the harmony that the animals had enjoyed now disappeared. Instead there was anxiety and fear, because, as some of them had foretold, the lion turned out to be a very cruel and unpredictable ruler with a ravenous appetite. Once he became king, he began killing and eating many of the smaller animals in the forest.

So afraid were the animals that none of them dared to say anything to the king. Although he held daily court, the lion did all the talking. Nobody disagreed with him, as questioning the king was very dangerous. All he cared about was having a full stomach. Whenever he pounced on and ate an unfortunate victim, the lion's excuse was that the animal had made a mistake, and mistakes of any kind were not allowed. After a while, the lion was killing so many of his fellow animals that he could no longer claim to be hungry. Instead, he had learned to enjoy killing for killing's sake. Now no animal in the kingdom was safe, from the smallest mouse to the mightiest elephant.

So bad was the animals' plight that one day the timid dik-dik antelope summoned the courage to call a secret meeting of all the animals. When they were gathered together, she said, "We wanted a ruler who would make the forest a better place, but we made a terrible mistake in choosing the lion. He terrorizes and exploits us and has killed and eaten hundreds of our friends. We must stop him, but how?"

The wise bonobo spoke up, saying, "We are many and the lion is only one. If we all pull together we can throw him out of the forest."

This was too much for the other animals, who were too afraid to attempt to overthrow the lion. But they agreed that the bonobo could go to the king and plead for mercy toward the other animals in the forest, so the bonobo set off for the lion's den.

Luckily, the lion, who was growing fatter and lazier by the day, had just eaten an unfortunate ostrich that had strayed into his sight, so he did not pounce on the bonobo as she approached. "What do you want, ape?" he growled.

The bonobo replied, "Your majesty, I am here to help you remember that a king does not need sharp teeth and claws and a mighty roar to rule wisely. A good king rules with compassion and humility. He makes sure his subjects are happy and safe. I beg you to stop killing and have mercy on your subjects."

The lion snarled with fury. "How dare you address your king in this way!" he roared. "You're lucky my belly is too full for me to move, otherwise I would kill and eat *you* right here and now."

The bonobo returned to the disappointed animals, having failed in her mission, and another meeting was held. The discussions continued long into the night until finally the hare said that she had a plan that might improve their lives. "The king enjoys killing so much that soon there will not be enough of us left to eat and he will starve to death. But he is also growing fat and lazy. I propose that we draw lots each day and whoever is unlucky enough to be the winner will be a meal for the king. This way, more of us will be saved and we can control the king's appetite and his anger." It was a terrible proposal, but none of the animals could think of a better plan and they all agreed to put it to the king.

That night, all the animals of the forest gathered in front of the lion's den. As they drew near, they could hear him gnawing on his latest victim, a fat kudu who had been so busy grazing it had not heard the lion creep up behind. The hare hopped carefully toward the lion, who licked his lips at the prospect of an additional evening snack. But just as he raised a huge paw, the hare said, "Your majesty, please hear me out. We have a plan that will make your life easier and mean that you need never be at the trouble of hunting again." And the hare explained the terrible plan she had devised to make sure the lion had a daily meal.

The lion didn't think it was a terrible plan at all. He very much liked the idea. His dinner would come to him instead of his having to go out and get it, and he would have even less to do. Ruling the kingdom was tiresome enough already. The hare's plan would give him more time to laze in the sun and sleep. So the lion said, "I agree to your proposal, but be sure that my dinner comes to me by sunset every day, otherwise I'll kill all of you."

After that, the animals in the forest held a lottery every day to determine who would be the lion's dinner and every day at sunset the poor animal would walk into the lion's den to be eaten.

Although life in the forest became predictable the animals were far from happy. Their terrible plan gave them more control, but all of them lived in fear that they would be the next winner of the dinner lottery and knew their turn would surely come. Once the daily draw was over, and the next victim chosen, the other animals would slink away in misery and tremble in fear for the rest of the day and night.

The lion was delighted with the arrangement. He no longer had to crawl around and hunt down his food. Now his dinner walked right up to meet him. Consequently, he grew fatter and fatter and lazier and lazier, and meanwhile the crops still failed, the rivers were still choked, and the trees of the forest fell all around him.

Nevertheless, the animals preferred their chosen misery to the alternative, and had no further thoughts of trying to overthrow King Lion until the day came when the bonobo was chosen to be his next meal. The bonobo didn't seem upset, as some other animals had been; neither was she in a hurry to have it over and done with, as others had felt. Instead, she busied herself in the forest, deliberately delaying her departure, and did not arrive at the lion's den until long after sunset. By then, the lion was in a very foul mood.

When he saw the bonobo, the lion bellowed, "Why have you kept me waiting so long? I could kill all of you for this!" The bonobo replied, "My deepest apologies, your majesty, but it is not my fault I am late. A lion was chasing me and wanted to eat me for dinner. I thought there was no other lion in the forest and I was astonished—why, sire, I believe he is even bigger, fiercer, and has a much louder roar than your majesty."

"What?" roared the lion. "Another lion has dared enter my forest? Where is he? I will tear him to pieces!"

The bonobo said, "I will show you the way and you shall see for yourself." And she set off, followed by the lion. They padded through the forest until they arrived at a deep well. The bonobo pointed to it, and said, "This is the place where the lion lives, your majesty. I believe it is hiding inside."

The lion crept up and looked down into the depths of the well. There, to his great surprise, he saw another lion. The sight made him furiously angry and he roared, and roared, and roared. But the other lion seemed to roar back even louder, as the king's voice echoed round the well. Provoked beyond endurance, the lion king pounced on his reflection, fell deep into the water of the well, and drowned.

When the bonobo returned, the other animals were terrified to see that she was still alive. Hadn't the king sworn to kill them all if he did not have his dinner? But when the bonobo told them how her trick had worked, and that the lion king was drowned and gone forever, they cheered and praised her cleverness. Then the porcupine rattled his quills until there was silence and said, "My friends, we wanted a ruler who would be clever, and look after us, and keep us safe. We made the wrong choice once, out of fear. Let us make the right choice now, with what we can see with our own eyes and hear with our own ears. I propose the bonobo should be our queen." All the other animals agreed unanimously.

"Thank you, my friends," said the bonobo. "From today I decree that there shall be no more killing in the forest. Tonight, let us celebrate our freedom from the tyranny of King Lion. But tomorrow I will hold court and invite every one of you to tell me what you think should be done to make our life in the forest better. I promise I will listen to what you have to say and that in as short a time as possible our land will bear ripe fruit and vegetables, our rivers will run clear and free, and our trees will grow tall and strong."

And just as the bonobo queen had promised, in no time at all life in the forest was transformed. Every animal was heard, from the tiniest shrew to the bulkiest rhinoceros, and all worked together to put the land to rights. The forest prospered and everything that grew and worked within it lived happily ever after.

To love and to work

When I wrote this story, I had a particular case in mind. It concerned Heal-Era, a health products company I had some knowledge of through my friendship with a member of the board. The leadership crisis Heal-Era faced almost brought the company down.

Ironically, Heal-Era, which was supposedly dedicated to wellbeing and life-enhancing products, was a deeply unhappy place to work, according to glassdoor.com, an online forum that gives people a chance to gossip about their jobs. The comments registered there made disturbing reading. Heal-Era came across as having a very unpleasant, toxic work environment. The glassdoor.com rating, on a scale from 1 to 5, put the company at a miserable 2. A common thread of the complaints was Heal-Era's Darwinian atmosphere: in the company, it was eat or be eaten. Other complaints included rude and inconsiderate management, the lack of educational opportunities, inconsiderate working hours (among other things, people were required to work on public holidays), and lack of respect for employees.

I had the impression that Heal-Era was steeped in paranoia and the depressive reactions that paranoia produces. I already knew the company had a super-aggressive attitude toward competitors. At the slightest sign of patent infringement, top management went into overdrive to start litigation. I was also aware that Heal-Era's fiercely competitive culture extended within the organization, as well as to outsiders, due to its very personalized bonus system. Because employees could make serious money by reaching their targets, they often went so far as to sabotage each other's work. And the annual purge of the bottom 10 percent of performers did nothing to help general morale in the company. Unsurprisingly, trust was non-existent and teamwork unknown. Instead, the words everybody in the company had drummed into them were "shareholder value," which was pursued at the cost of anything else. This preoccupation explained the austerity and cheapness of the way the company dealt with its people.

The CEO of this toxic company was Norman Sentry. So what was he like? Most decisions were taken single-handedly by Norman. He didn't believe in giving people voice or considering other people's opinions. In fact, he tended to treat everyone who worked in the company, at all levels, like helpless children. His attitude toward them was patronizing at best, and clearly he trusted none of them, a feeling that was mutual. Most of his employees regarded him with a mixture of dread and awe. But—and it was a big but that helped explain why he was still there—Norman seemed to know how to make money for the company.

Norman's reign was eventually brought to an end by a pollution scandal. It was not only the atmosphere within the company that was toxic: Heal-Era had been cutting corners in dealing with its waste products and polluting the environment around its various plants. When the scandal hit the media, Heal-Era's share price tumbled significantly, raising serious questions about Norman's leadership. A number of suits and counter-suits followed. As bad news piled on bad news, the board had no choice but to force Norman to resign. Subsequently, it brought in a prominent businesswoman, Vera Broome, to clean up the mess.

Vera realized when she accepted the job that a change of corporate culture would take time, as paranoia is not easily cured. She knew that changing the mindset of the people in the company would require a great deal of effort on her part. But in contrast to her predecessor, she realized that leaders do not only affect financial performance indicators; they also affect the mental wellbeing of the people they lead. Vera understood the importance of values and culture.

The first thing Vera did was to take out what she called "the rotten apples"—people who had been the ringleaders in creating and perpetuating Heal-Era's toxic corporate culture. She got rid of the old bonus system and introduced a much fairer, team-based reward structure, making it very clear that people who didn't live the company's new values would have no future there. She also added non-financial benefits to the package, including educational opportunities. Decision-making would be decentralized. Vera wanted to do away with the top-down mentality. She wanted, in her words, to "tap people's brains," not have a culture of passive dependency.

Within a few years, glassdoor.com was rating Heal-Era at 4.5, a highly satisfying result for Vera. The rating was recognition of a great deal of hard work and a major culture change within the organization. Clearly, Vera had been highly effective in designing the kind of organizational systems, teams, and culture that helped everyone in the company succeed and thrive.

Many leaders, as the story of King Lion illustrates, have no idea how to create a place where everyone will give their best. Instead, they create misery for others. Under such leadership, the workplace turns into a place of fear, characterized by an atmosphere where people are preoccupied in covering their own backs, making for a blame-oriented culture. Organizations like this are not known for their creativity. On the contrary, they produce stress, contribute to illness, and are marked by under-performance, absenteeism, and high staff turnover. There are many horror stories about how such dysfunctional organizations induce depressive reactions, alcoholism, substance abuse, and other stress disorders among their people.

Yet organizations do not need to be stressful. On the contrary, organizations can be anchors of psychological wellbeing: ways of establishing identity and maintaining self-esteem. They could be bastions of mental health. Freud once suggested that mental health depends on "*lieben und arbeiten,"* our ability to love and work. We invest the organizations to which we belong with a considerable amount of psychological meaning. Accomplishing something tangible through our work brings stability to a highly unstable world. Organization means putting things in order; by extension, organizations could be ideal environments for helping us to cope with the stresses and strains of our daily life, rather than inducing them.

The psychological contract

The moral of the tale of King Lion is about creating a healthy place to live and work, which the wise bonobo accomplished. What does the tale tell us about what leaders can do to contribute to the wellbeing of their people?

For very fundamental reasons, healthy people need healthy environments. As our tale about the animal kingdom demonstrates, this sort of organizational ambiance is created by inspirational leadership, excellent working conditions, and a sense of purpose. A healthy environment is a place where the people trust their leaders, have pride in their work and company, and have a sense of camaraderie. The forest that King Lion reigned over was very far from this ideal.

Organizations have always been important navigation points in a sea of change. Belonging to an organization can be a way of coping with economic and social upheaval, a fixed point in turbulent times. As the economist John Kenneth Galbraith observed, "All of the great leaders have had one characteristic in common: it was the willingness to confront unequivocally the major anxiety of their people in their time."

Increasingly, however, executives have become independent agents, less attached to the organization, and organizational identification and loyalty have become far less important. Very few people nowadays join an organization and expect to spend the rest of their working life within it. For many, the psychological contract between employer and organization has been broken.

This can have a profound negative effect. Organizations used to provide a "holding environment" for their people, containing anxiety through the agency of their leaders. Nowadays, however, organizations seem to be less prepared to take on this function. The loss of the psychological contract has made the work situation more stressful, a development that does not augur well for employees' mental health. Yet unhealthy organizations will not thrive; indeed, the life cycle of organizations has become shorter and shorter. So what can organizational leaders do to make their companies healthier places to work?

In fact, there are many things organizations can do to create a healthy environment in which their people can thrive and which they will be motivated to keep healthy. Organizational leadership may subscribe to practices such as stock option plans, profit-sharing systems, no layoff policies, non-hierarchical structures, information-sharing systems, flexible hours, and casual dress codes. They may hold events that help to create a sense of community. They may provide state-of-the-art fitness centers, leisure facilities, on-site clinics, on-site childcare, cafeterias with great food, and generous health insurance policies. These organizations are usually also very family friendly, which basically means women friendly. The companies that score high on this kind of list go to great lengths to create organizational cultures that have a positive effect on mental health.

All these things have to be based on a firm foundation of values and beliefs that define an organization's fundamental purpose and culture. These values and beliefs need to be articulated clearly and forcefully on every possible occasion. In our tale, the first thing the bonobo does on becoming ruler is to state a new law ("There shall be no more killing") and promise a new culture of openness and trust ("I invite every one of you to tell me what you think should be done to make our life in the forest better"). And, the tale tells us, she keeps her word and life does become better for the animals of the forest. Importantly, she gives the animals voice and the opportunity for self-determination, something that was clearly missing under the rule of King Lion.

Important though these values and beliefs are, the very best places to work provide three further essential ingredients in the form of meta-values that respond to our motivational needs systems: love, fun, and meaning. This implies creating a sense of belonging, a sense of enjoyment, and a sense of meaning.

I have coined a term to describe these more enlightened organizations: I refer to them as *authentizotic*. This term is derived from two Greek words: *authenteekos* and *zoteekos*. The first conveys the idea that the organization is authentic, while *zoteekos* means "vital to life." In these organizations, people feel complete and alive. In the very non-authentizotic environment of the forest, under the rule of King Lion, of course, staying alive took on a whole different meaning.

In my view, the biggest challenge for leaders today is to create authentizotic organizations that provide an antidote to stress and a healthier existence, contributing to a more fulfilling life. In these organizations, employees can maintain an effective balance between personal and organizational life and continue to learn from experience.

There is an old proverb that says: a smart man learns from his experience, but a wise man learns from the experiences of others. For much of our lives we do not give enough thought to our significant emotional experiences. We busy about our daily activities without thinking about their meaning, surrounded by a mass of undigested experiences. We need to deal with these experiences as creatively as possible, but it is difficult to do that if our boss is a King Lion.

As the US politician Geraldine Ferraro famously said, "Some leaders are born women." Getting things done is an essential characteristic of effective leadership. In our story, the bonobo's natural talent for leadership is obvious from when she first speaks, but her fellow animals are too daunted by King Lion to recognize her wisdom and courage. So the bonobo, who knows what needs to be done to bring the reign of King Lion to an end, waits for the opportune moment to demonstrate her leadership qualities.

The tale of the Bear-King showed that a solid dose of humility is a great boon to any leader. Similarly, the bonobo recognizes that to command is to serve and attempted to make King Lion grasp that point. She also realizes that someone who has great power should use it lightly and, when her turn comes, makes it clear that she will be the kind of leader who will lead by example. The moral of this fairy tale is that if leaders want to have a prosperous forest, they will do better to behave like the bonobo, rather than the lion. People cannot rule others if they cannot govern themselves.

Coaching culture test

The following questions measure the degree to which you are working in a coaching-oriented organization. Answer them with *Yes* or *No*.

1. Is open communication important in your organization?
2. Is trust a key quality of your organization?
3. Does your organization have an ongoing commitment to learning and development?
4. Does your organization have a team-oriented culture?
5. Do the people in your organization celebrate work well done?
6. Do people have voice in your organization?
7. Is constructive feedback an ongoing process?
8. Does your organization provide you with room to be creative?
9. Do you have a strong sense of belonging in your organization?
10. Does your work give you meaning?
11. Do you get much enjoyment out of your work?
12. Do you subscribe to the core values and mission of your organization?
13. Do you feel well rewarded in your work?
14. Does your organization get the best out of you?
15. Do you have confidence in your organization's leadership?

The more you answer *Yes*, the higher your score. If you score high, you are fortunate to work in a coaching, authentizotic organization. If you score low, however, your company probably would not feature on a list of best places to work.

Why is it that, although authentizotic organizations seem so desirable when seen from outside, and so pleasant from within, so few organizations can claim to have this kind of organizational culture? Why are working relationships so often dysfunctional? Why are so many executive teams ineffectual? Some answers may lie in human nature—our tendency to trust one another so far, and no further—and our inability to see past our own needs to understand that richer psychological and material benefits might be easier to obtain through team efforts than on our own. This is not easy to accept, let alone change. When teamwork is based on trust, we are more comfortable and more productive. Organizations with a coaching culture operate like networked webs, connecting people laterally in the same departments, across departments, between teams, and up and down the hierarchy.

chapter

7

Happy Ever After

He who lives in harmony with himself lives in harmony with the universe.

—Marcus Aurelius

If you are without kindness, you will meet no kindness in return.

—Tibetan proverb

Deeper meaning resides in the fairy tales told to me in my childhood than in the truth that is taught by life.

—Friedrich Schiller

Explorations of the interior

The mythologist Joseph Campbell wrote in his seminal work, *The Hero With a Thousand Faces*: "The happy ending of the fairy tale, the myth, and the divine comedy of the soul, is to be read, not as a contradiction, but as a transcendence of the universal tragedy of man." These fairy tales illustrate the five deadly dangers of leadership and highlight various ways in which leaders can derail. I contend that only by confronting these dangers head on can people in leadership positions grow emotionally and spiritually.

At the heart of each of these five fairy tales is a personal developmental task: As the protagonists leave their old lives behind and enter the unknown, to face and eventually conquer the various challenges they face, they are expected to develop their highest potential. Therefore, for the heroes and heroines in these fairy tales, the quest is first and foremost an inner journey to discover what they are all about, and what truly matters to them. Through this process of self-examination they will discover the inner awareness that enables them to lead.

My primary aim in presenting these fairy tales for the boardroom is to emphasize that mastering the art of leadership comes with mastery of the self. Developing leadership is a process of self-developing. To conquer the self, as these five fairy tales demonstrate, leaders should not shy away from difficult personal challenges. Only through meeting these challenges head on will they grow emotionally and spiritually.

The tales in this book also show that developing leadership capabilities is about much more than learning the latest management theories. A leader does not just need the right number of the right tools. To be an effective leader, we need to recognize our own unique capabilities and passions. This implies that we have to learn how to use ourselves as sounding boards for those around us, be in tune with our surroundings, and understand others and ourselves. To be able to demonstrate authentic leadership we need to be in tune with our inner world. Only when we know what we want to do, and why we want to do it, will we be able to feel good about ourselves. The quests of the characters in these fairy tales should appeal to the hero in us all. I hope these stories will encourage willing leaders to embark on their own inner quest and make a difference in one way or another.

We probably all remember that when we were children we thought we were destined to do or be something special. We wanted to be unique in some way. Those feelings of specialness never completely dissipate. As adults, we need to be recognized and feel we can make meaningful contributions. These fairy tales may have left us with symbolic, subliminal messages that are not always be easy to read or may even go unnoticed.

Some may read these stories and take them simply at face value, as fairy tales. Others may respond to their symbolism.

All five tales borrow from the conventions of traditional fairy tales, which in turn have their roots in ancient myths. I have intentionally loaded these adventures with symbolic material, in the hope that readers who are touched (consciously or unconsciously) by their symbolism might develop a deeper awareness of themselves. My intention has been that these tales should contain more than meets the eye, as well as entertaining their readers.

In the opening chapter of this book, I described how children learn how to overcome psychological conflicts and grow into new phases of development through their symbolic understanding of the maturation process, as expressed in fairy tales. This is one of the main points made by the child psychologist Bruno Bettelheim, in his book *The Uses of Enchantment: The Meaning and Importance of Fairy Tales*, first published in 1976. Bettelheim suggests that fairy tales are existential dramas in which children subconsciously confront their own problems and desires on the path to adulthood. Fairy tales help them to answer basic existential questions, like "Who am I?," "What is the good life?," "Where do I belong?," "How do I make the right choices?," and "What is my calling?" Because fairy tales use symbolic language, they help children discover their identity, their calling, and what they need to do to develop their character further. Thus, while fairy tales do not literally represent the external world, they capture the inner world that a young child does not have language or cognitive structures to understand or control. Through fairy tales, children learn to navigate reality and survive in a world full of dangers.

Given the early imprinting of fairy tales in the human psyche, my hope is that the five tales I present here will retain their power for an adult readership and will still capture my readers' imagination. The existential questions we struggle with as children remain into adulthood. Most of us will struggle to define and redefine ourselves as we go through major life transitions or upheavals. The ancient Delphic injunction to "Know thyself" resonates down the ages. We cannot make successful transitions in our life without knowing who we are and what we really want.

The fairy tale as a psychological mirror

In these five stories I have tried to show that fairy tales are psychological mirrors. At first they seem to reflect only our own image, but behind that image we soon discover our inner turmoil and ways to gain peace with ourselves and the world. Our understanding of fairy tales becomes more complex as we mature and recognize in them familiar existential crises and deep truths.

I hope the truths dramatized in these five tales will resonate with leaders in any context, as well as the boardroom. Their brevity, themes, and treatment of magical events should allow them to be interpreted, reinterpreted, and expanded upon whoever the reader may be. My aim in writing them has been to help readers understand their environment and their personal difficulties better, and to guide their actions.

My wish is that the psychological healing process at the heart of these five fairy tales will be a source of inspiration for every reader. The models of the hero or heroine in these tales, who struggles and eventually succeeds by taking resolute action, may stimulate emerging leaders to do the same. Although these fairy tales take us into imaginary realms, peopled with talking animals and a variety of monstrous beings, I think readers will see that I have maintained a strong connection with the real world throughout their telling.

The tales provide insights about how leaders might deal with the five deadly dangers they face. In identifying with the characters in these stories we may come to understand our own internal struggles between good and evil. From an existential point of view, all these stories declare that the happy ever after is achievable. Virtue is rewarded, vice and foolishness are punished, and the weak become strong.

The most enduring question in philosophy, religion and psychology is about the meaning of life. In the words of Mark Twain, "The two most important days in your life are the day you are born and the day you find out why." In life, what really matters is that we have the chance to be what we are, and to become what we are capable of becoming. One of the greatest human fears is that at the end of our life we might discover that we have never really lived. We all have the urge to live fully, to do something significant, and to make a difference. Our biggest challenge is to work out how to do it. In summing up, my hope in writing this small book of fairy tales for the board room is that it may provide the reader with a modicum of insight of how to make a difference—and in the process, how to become an effective leader and learn how to avoid the five major dangers of leadership.

Bibliography

In devising the five tales in this book I was very much influenced by *The Nights of Straparola* by Giovanni Francesco Straparola. Generally considered the father of the literary fairy tale in Europe, Straparola was an Italian writer and poet who lived around 1480–1558. His major contribution is *Le piacevoli notti*, translated variously as *The Pleasant Nights*, *The Entertaining Nights*, *The Facetious Nights*, or *The Delectable Nights*. The tales in this collection are told over 13 consecutive nights by a group of men and women gathered at a Venetian palace. Straparola's tales influenced many other writers, including Giambattista Basile, Charles Perrault, and the Brothers Grimm.

Another influence was the *One Thousand and One Nights*, folktales of largely Middle Eastern and Indian origin, including the tales of Aladdin, Ali Baba, and Sinbad the Sailor, which have almost become part of Western folklore. The premise of this collection is that the sultan Shahrayar discovers that his wife has been unfaithful. He kills her and vows to marry a different woman every night and kill her the next morning to prevent any further betrayal. When he takes Scheherazade as his bride, she devises a scheme of saving herself by telling the sultan a tale every night, but leaving the story unfinished, promising to complete it the following night. The stories are so entertaining and so enchanting, and the king so eager to hear the ending, that he continually postpones her death.

Similar influences were Giambattista Basile's *Stories from the Pentamerone*, published in two volumes in Naples, Italy, in 1634 and 1636, and the classic retelling of many well-loved tales by Charles Perrault (1697).

However, my biggest influence in writing these stories was *Grimms' Fairy Tales*. The stories collected by Jacob and Wilhelm Grimm in the early 1800s serve up life as generations of central Europeans knew it—capricious and often cruel. The brothers studied the folklore of their region and recorded oral storytelling, which was vanishing fast with the advent of new printing technology. The brothers' work culminated in *Children's and Household Tales*, the first volume of which was published in 1812. Once they realized how the tales fascinated young readers, the Grimms, and many editors after them, started to "sanitize" the stories, which gradually became gentler and sweeter, and (like my five stories) contained a strong moral message. The stories were reprinted many times, and the collection grew from 86 to more than 200. The final collection represented an amalgamation of oral and previously published fairy tales, as well as information shared by friends, family members, and acquaintances, with non-German influences.

Finally, my travels have taken me around the world and brought me into close contact with people of many nations. I have been particularly influenced by African, American Indian, and Siberian folk tales, in which tricksters and animals play a central role. As well as entertaining their listeners, these stories teach moral lessons about survival.

Index

Aesop's Fables, 2
altruism, 90
Andersen, Hans Christian
    tale of *The Emperor's New Clothes*,
        12–13
anger, 76
Aristotle, on self-knowledge, 28
arrogance, 50, 52, 53, 55, 61
assertiveness, 54
authenticity in action, 31
authentizotic organization, 113, 114

Bacon, Francis, 34
Bettelheim, Bruno
    *The Uses of Enchantment: The
        Meaning and Importance of Fairy
        Tales*, 118
boastfulness, 50
Brothers Grimm, 2, 121, 122

Campbell, Joseph
    *The Hero With a Thousand
        Faces*, 116
Churchill, Winston, 76
coaching
    culture of, 102–15
    culture test, 114
    for leadership, 77–8
    team, 91, 96–9

conceit, 50
confidence, 37, 54
creativity, 54, 60, 100, 110

denial, 30
developmental journeys, 74–6
dream imagery, 11–12
dysfunctional teams, 94–5

ego, 53
Einstein, Albert, 100
emotional stinginess, 77
encouragement, 73, 77, 78
envy, 13, 18, 23, 34–6, 55, 58
extrinsic motivation, 72, 73

fables, 4
fairy tale, 6–12
    Bear King, 38–61, 113
    Beauty and the Beast, 32
    dream imagery, 11–12
    The Emperor's New Clothes, 12–13
    Four Brothers, 80
    Kindly Crone, 62
    King Lion, 102
    in leader's journey, 12–14
    personal transformation, 9–10
    as psychological mirror, 119–20
    Snow White, 13, 32

fairy tale – continued
   structural patterns of, 7–9
   symbolism, 10–12
   The Uses of Enchantment: The
      Meaning and Importance of Fairy
      Tales, 118
   White Raven, 17–25, 27, 31–4
feedback, 30, 31, 99
   constructive, 37, 59
Ferraro, Geraldine, 113
forgiveness, 76

Gaddafi, Muammar, 52
Galbraith, John Kenneth, 111
Goethe, 78
Golem effect, 76
grandiosity, 54, 55
greed, 5, 35, 55
groupthink, 53, 95, 98

Hitler, Adolf, 52
hubris, 14, 38–61
   preventive measures of, 57–60
   test, 60–1

interior, explorations of, 116–18
intrinsic motivation, 72, 73

Johari Window matrix of self-
      knowledge, 30–1
Jung, Carl, 10–11

"know thyself," 25–9, 118

La Fontaine, 2
leaders, following, 90–3
leadership, 12–14, 80–101
   coaching for, 77–8
   complementarities of, 88–9
   dangers of, 14–16

developing, 117
organizational, 112
social connection and, 89–90
as team sport, 87–9
Lord Acton, 57

me generation, 53
micromanagement, 75
Milton
   Paradise Lost, 52
mirroring, 32–3
Molière (Monsieur Jourdain)
   Le Bourgeois Gentilhomme, 3
motivation, 62–79
   conundrum, 70–4
   extrinsic, 72, 73
   intrinsic, 72, 73
   test, 78–9

narcissism, 53–6
   essential characteristics of, 54
   excessive, 55, 58
   preventive measures of, 57–60
narcissists
   constructive versus reactive, 54
   self-confidence of, 56
Narcissus in Greek myth, story of, 32

passivity, 56
personal gratification, 53
personal transformation, 9–10
Plato
   on self-knowledge, 28
pomposity, 55
power, 12, 13, 57, 58, 96
praise, 77
pride, 52, 53, 111
pseudo-team, 91
psychological contract, 111–14
Pygmalion effect, 76–7

rage, 39–41, 50, 55
repetition, 12
resentment, 75, 76
resistance to criticism, 53
role modeling, 77

Saint-Exupéry, Antoine de, 73
Schadenfreude, 10, 35
self-appraisal, 28
self-awareness mirror test, 36–7
self-centeredness, 50, 54
self-deception, 27, 34
self-delusion, 26, 53
self-enhancement, 51
self-esteem, 29, 54, 55, 59–60,
      89, 110
self-fulfillment, 53, 76
self-importance, 39, 52
self-imprisonment, 53
self-knowledge, 14, 17–25, 27, 52,
      33–6, 52
   Aristotle on, 28
   Johari Window matrix of, 30–1
   Plato on, 28
self-love, 53, 54
self-mortification, 31
Shakespeare
   Othello, 52

social connection, and leadership, 89–90
Socrates
   on self-knowledge, 28
Sophocles
   Oedipus Rex, 28–9, 52
specialness, 55, 59, 117
spitefulness, 55, 55
storytelling, 4–5, 14
structural patterns of fairy tale, 7–9
symbolism, 7, 10–11, 118

team(s)
   attraction of, 89–93
   coaching, *see* team coaching
   dysfunctional, 94–5
   pseudo-team, 91
team coaching, 91, 96–9
   execution of, 97–8
   undiscussables, 98–9
   vulnerabilities of, 99–100
teambuilding test, 100
Thales of Miletus
   on self-knowledge, 28
Twain, Mark, 75, 119

vindictiveness, 35, 40, 55

Zafón, Carlos Ruiz, 35